How selling wieners, being myself, and a few easy-to-copy steps were the launching point for my career and can teach anybody how to thrive and not just survive in sales, marketing, business ownership and any career they love. Not just in the digital age but for decades to come.

By Mike Rudd

To my wife Jill, you are the love of my life.
Here's to good friends, tonight's kinda special,
ching!

"Our lives begin to end the day we become silent about things that matter."

Dr. Martin Luther King Jr.

"Many of life's failures are people who did not realize how close they were to success when they gave up."

Thomas Edison

"The big win is when you refuse to settle for average or mediocre."

Seth Godin

"And if you wait around until the weekend then you miss the best things to do."

James Murphy aka LCD Soundsystem

"I've missed more than 9000 shots in my career. I've lost almost 300 games. 26 times, I've been trusted to take the game winning shot and missed. I've failed over and over and over again in my life. And that is why I succeed."
Michael Jordan

Foreword

The first thing you need to know about this book is that it wasn't written for you.

It's pretty apparent to anyone reading these pages that Mike isn't trying to take on the burden of training the next generation of salespeople or reinventing the marketing industry; he's simply recording his personal experiences, insights, and lessons from his still adolescent career in these fields. Every personal development book tells you that it is impossible to dramatically improve your lot in life unless you take the time to analyze your past actions and results. And Mike is in a constant state of improvement.

The revelation of this fact came to me after reading the conclusions at the end of the first few chapters. I'd originally thought that the two or three "Carry Out" points would be bite-sized lessons I could take away from the chapter and personally put into action. It turns out they ARE the most important lessons in the chapter, but specific to the author's experience. The bullet points are the valuable experiences Mike learned from the story. But in reading Mike's observations, I could also identify the personal takeaways for myself. Mike sharing his insights allowed me to add my own Carry Out bullet points in order to make the stories (and lessons) more applicable to my own situation. I think you'll find the same benefit.

The second thing you need to know about the book is that like all the best hot dogs – this book is all meat. Mike's stories and their personal impact is USDA Grade-A 100% all-beef.

Absolutely zero filler.

Mike has provided us with his personal lessons all the way from his first "real" job in sales, up to his current role as the top salesperson in his chosen field. The only trick here is that it is impossible for this book to be filled with the lessons and experiences of a lifetime in sales and marketing. You see, Mike isn't even close to the end of his career. It's quite the opposite – Mike is just at the beginning of what will surely be an incredibly successful personal and professional life.

My hope is that this book is simply the first of several volumes sharing the experiences and lessons and insights gained from that life. He'd be in good company. P.T. Barnum and Benjamin Franklin both crafted their memoirs over decades. Barnum published a few books, each containing portions of his life and personal advice. Franklin crafted his autobiography into four distinct sections to mirror the stages of his career.

Take and consume the hot dogs and advice Mike is serving you within this book, but don't just learn from Mike's story. Add your own toppings to the hot dog. If you build your own experiences into the lessons he shares in this book, you can bet your buns that you'll get more out of it and it will help you get the success you crave by feeding your mind.

Now, turn the page and bite into the juicy ideas contained inside – get 'em while they're hot!

~Don The Idea Guy Snyder

August 28, 2012

Appetizers

The title says it all. How did I make it into the cutthroat world of 100% commission sales? In an industry that some pundits proclaimed would be dead before the time I graduated from college? Not only make it, but turn it into a career?

A career that I love, get excited for every day I wake up, and love to be a part of?

By simply combining hot dogs, a little dash of marketing, and a plethora of fun into my everyday life. That is how it happened!

When I set off for The Ohio State University the third Saturday in September of 2001, I was an undecided major. I had no job prospects for my freshman year, and not really a clue of where I wanted to go in life. I was not a mess by any stretch of the imagination, but I certainly could have used a bit more dedication and aspirations for the future.

My father and I had a pretty telling talk on the way up from Cincinnati to move me into the dorm. Boston was playing from the speakers of the mini van, and we did not see eye to eye on where I was headed.

Well, we saw eye to eye that we were driving to Columbus, just not where I was headed in the long term and in my overall life.

He was right. I needed to figure it out. And I thank him for letting me know that I wasn't headed to Ohio State just to party, hang out, and watch football games. Those B's in high school weren't going to turn into C's in college on my parents' watch.

But when he left that day, I was on my own. It was time to man up.

It was time to really get focused, and I was entering a world changing so rapidly that if you blinked you were sure to miss something. Facebook, Twitter, and LinkedIn would be developed while I was in college. We were among the first graduating classes entering into a terrible job market that turned into a "recession or mini depression" some say still exists. The tragedy of 9/11 had just occurred and I had no idea what was in store for our country. The entire educational and healthcare systems were being questioned, and I was entering into a world that was changing so rapidly every day that it was sink or swim time.

And I wanted to swim.

I wanted to swim extraordinarily far and ridiculously fast.

My swim started then and continues today with three simple ingredients (actually, goggles would be necessary too):

1) Hot Dogs
2) A Little Marketing
3) A Lot of Fun

Chapter 1: BUNS

Yes, I have seen every single condiment that the chapters of this book are named after placed onto a hot dog at one time or another.

No ifs, ands, or BUNS about it. People like interesting things on their hot dogs.

I guess it didn't start with hot dogs immediately after I fell onto the Ohio State campus. My freshman year, which was *A* pluses all around when it came to grades, fun, and meeting new people, was off to a great start. I was taking the core classes that any college student needs, so even though I was undecided about my major, I wasn't losing any progress toward graduating on time.

Undecided turned into a major during spring quarter. I was talking to Reid, one of the three OSU soccer players who bunked in the dorm room next to mine, and Reid mentioned he was in the business school for marketing.

I asked Reid, "Why did you choose marketing?"

Reid replied, "I want to work for Budweiser and design and write their TV and magazine ads."

I thought that sounded like a great career choice! (Little did I know that is actually Budweiser's advertising agency's job and purpose. I hope Reid figured that out too and his dreams weren't crushed.)

So, I applied and was accepted into the Fisher College of Business, planning a double major in marketing and logistics.

I was on the path to success!

Except I needed to start making some money as sophomore year started and I moved out of the dorm into my own place (not my own if you count the eight lovely friends that lived in the six-bedroom house with me), and funds were starting to dwindle.

I had worked two jobs the whole summer and saved a ton of cash. The problem was it all went to my tuition. The good news was I hadn't had to take a student loan out yet. The bad news was I needed money and I needed a job.

All the progress I had made over the past year in getting my life moving full speed ahead would suddenly hit an abrupt and screeching halt if I didn't figure out some cash flow in the form of a part-time job around my class schedule.

Carry Out (aka Summary Points or the To Go Doggie Bag!)

1) Working in marketing at Budweiser would be sweet.

2) Working all summer only to send money to the school you go to is sort of a buzz kill as it's happening, but it's great when you are graduated and don't have mounds of student debt.

Chapter 2: ROASTED RED PEPPERS

The hot dogs, as I was about to say in Chapter 1 but went off on a tangent about my freshmen year, actually began with a yellow 3M Post it Note.

All the Post-it said was "Change Makers Wanted. $10 an hour cash free lunch."

The Post-it note was stuck to the food cart of Boss Doggs owner and my soon-to-be-employer, Eric Clark.

Boss Doggs was the B O M B to say the least! In a campus full of subpar dining halls, Boss Doggs had three carts on campus every day offering up grilled dogs, brats, chicken fajitas, sandwiches, and drinks. Sometimes they say you find a place when you are least looking for it, and that certainly was so. I wasn't even remotely looking. I was sitting at home studying when my friend Drew came over and said, "I talked to Boss Doggs, I think you got a job there. His name is Eric. Go see him at the Hitchcock Hall food cart. You start tomorrow 10:00 a.m."

And that was that.

Eric hired me once he realized I could count (I was to be a change maker for him – the only two math skills I needed to be decent at were fifth-grade-level addition and subtraction), could speak English, and wasn't creepy (he was going to have me standing at his side four hours a day five days a week.) No need to hire a weirdo to be his wingman.

And with that I had a job!

Money issues could at least be put off and rent would be getting paid without having to make a call down to the 'rents in Cincinnati on the 30th of each month.

Here is my first lesson from what I learned about hot dogs that would help me in my career.

Attitude.

Eric, the owner of Boss Doggs, had an attitude that everyone on Ohio State campus knew about.

It wasn't a bad thing either.

Eric had the attitude that today was a great day. And there wasn't anything you could do to tell him otherwise. He was known among Ohio State students as the guy who ran the hot dog cart who whistled all day long. He whistled happy tunes, songs, and melodies that you could hear as you passed from class to class.

Throw in the fact that his whistle also meant you could smell the sweet aroma of his fresh food on the grill, and it was a friendly reminder that maybe life wasn't so hard or so bad that day. After all the hot dog guy was whistling.

The second thing I learned about attitude and making what you can out of each day was that unless we were looking at a Mt. Everest summit type of windstorm, he was rocking shorts!

January, June, October, December - IT DID NOT MATTER.

The shorts were on, and he gave off the vibe that it was just another warm day in So Cal no matter the conditions.

I picked this up about Eric by the end of my first week as his "change maker."

By the time week one at Boss Doggs was in the books, I had accrued the followings items:

A) $200 in cash for my hourly wages
B) Five days of free lunch and bottled water
C) The lesson that attitude is everything and the day is what you make out of it. If you are happy and whistle, it will be a fun day. If you are wearing shorts, then in your world it will be warm.

Needless to say, it was a great start.

When I showed up for week two, Eric told me I would be working with the new guy and his cart a few blocks over on Wednesdays and Fridays.

Those Wednesdays and Fridays for the next two or so weeks would teach me everything I needed to know about how to garner good tips, the power of customer service and a quality product, and how to deal marijuana poorly if I ever felt the desire.

Oh, and it would lead to me getting to run my very own hot dog cart.

Carry Out

1) Yes, Drew, that Italian buddy of mine from college who looks like he should be on an episode of Jersey Shore, thought of the idea that I should work at Boss Doggs.

2) Best job interview ever was with Boss Doggs. It couldn't have been more than thirty seconds in length.

Chapter 3: CELERY SALT

I showed up on my first Wednesday with Dan (name changed to preserve his legacy at the Bier Stube on OSU campus) and found Dan to have his hot dog cart in a "hot mess."

I had been working with Eric the past few weeks learning about attitude and the ins and outs of the business. Basically Eric owned the business and if you worked for him on the cart, it was a 100% commission job. But you knew because of his exclusive food cart contract (for a nice sum paid to OSU each year) that you would have quite a bit of built-in business.

But how you grew that business and made it better was part you and part weather. Sunny days meant more drinks sales, bottom line. But you controlled the rest.

Eric kept his cart clean as can be and organized to a T. Dan did not gain this trait in his week-long training for his own Boss Doggs cart.

Hot dog bun packages were ripped open everywhere, there were too many dogs on the grill at once, and the peppers and onions for the fajitas were either burnt or soggy.

I did my best as "change maker" to organize Dan's station, but I could only do so much.

As we got to working, he started talking to me about how he had gotten loaded at the Bier Stube (my favorite bar still on OSU campus, I will say) until 2:00 a.m. the night before and barely made it in to work that day.

Keep in mind this is his new full-time job, he is 34, the Bier Stube is a college bar, and it was a Tuesday night.

I started to pick up on what I was dealing with, and it didn't shock me in the least when two college kids came over and bought $50 worth of marijuana from him, which he had hidden safely in plastic baggies in the bin where you store sanitation gloves, lighters, and the first aid kit.

Dan then proceeded to offer to sell me some, which I declined. Then he said that if I wanted to put out feelers in the hot dog line when I was making change to let him know and he could do a side deal real quick.

The hot dog cart had anywhere from three to twenty people in line from 10:45 a.m. until 2:00 p.m. every day. I discovered the faster you kept the line flowing – these students sometimes needed a quick bite between two classes and only had ten minutes – the more these kids would come back.

Slow lines, minimal repeat business.

And that is another takeaway for sales and marketing in our digital age. Don't expect repeat business if you make your customers feel anything but exhilarated that they are doing business with you.

Dan's desire to do side deals of marijuana after serving someone a hot dog began to slow the line down incredibly. He wasn't having any luck and didn't sell a lick of it all day; partly because I highly discouraged it and wasn't helping in the process of his side deals. Eric ran his business on the up and up and the last thing I wanted to do was have him get in trouble with the university. I kindly told Dan that if he brought the marijuana back the next day I would have to involve Eric. He must have thought I was the dorkiest college kid in history but I thought that wasn't the time or the place for his operation.

Dan couldn't figure out how after just one week his business and his tips had decreased each day.

I can tell you. Dan didn't pay attention to his core customers (the hot dog people) and instead worried about how I was preventing him from making an extra $65 each day by selling skanky weed to college kids by telling him to keep the weed at home.

Dan's tips decreased each day because he wasn't worried about delivering a quality product with a smile on his face and instead would turn over soggy peppers and onions or hot dogs that were either burnt or not cooked all the way through.

So while my three shifts with Dan as his change maker were a laughing train-wreck reality show in terms of how he was conducting business and reflecting on the Boss Doggs name, the good news was he was making money from built-in business that showed up every day.

It was enough money to go party at the Bier Stube like a rock star every night.

And when you party like a rock star every night until 2:30 a.m., it is really hard to get to work for your 7:00 a.m. job.

Dan missed work four days in a row his third week without calling.

Dan got fired.

Eric asked if I wanted to run my own cart on the fifth day, a Friday, which was by far our slowest day because college kids don't go to class on Friday. He said if I liked it and did it well, I could have my own cart and begin working full-time for him the following week. All my classes started at 3:30 p.m. or later, so the 7:00 a.m. to 3:00 p.m. shift fit perfectly into my day.

A full-time job outside, selling hot dogs, getting to see my friends on campus as they stopped by every day, free food, potentially good pay, and working for a guy who "gets it."

That sounded like a great gig to me.

Thanks, Dan. The Bier Stube thanks you too for the business.

Carry Out

1) The Bier Stube is and always will be the best bar on OSU Campus.

2) Sometimes things just fall into place.

Chapter 4: DICED TOMATOES

After a few weeks on the job, I realized I did not know nearly as much about the hot dog business as I had been inclined to think I did when I started.

I had my own cart, but it was a work in progress, with many things that took time to learn.

Determining the right level of flame on the pilot light to heat the water but not boil it too much. The amount of ice needed to cool the drinks on a hot day. How crispy the outside of a brat needed to be so the inside was cooked all the way through. And so on.

But each day as I went out there my first year, I learned.

I learned that if I had a smile on my face and was in a good mood, things went along easier and smoother that day.

I started to remember customers' names and their usual orders.

The more I started to call out to them by name or start making their orders as they came up, the more I started to receive tips.

They started to bring their friends.

We talked about classes we had together, we talked about the football team and that new coach in his second year named Tressel and how they could probably win the national title again in 2003 after they did so during that 2002 season. (They did not and have not won the title since 2002. Treasure your teams in the big moments even if they don't win. You never know when they will be there again.)

I hired my girlfriends Little Katie, Christie, and Suzie (nope, "ladies that are just friends", I was not like the guy on *Sister Wives* for all you reality TV junkies out there) as my change makers, and my lines kept moving faster and quicker.

If it was almost closing time and I had food left, I would do deals on the food to sell out and not have it go bad but still make a profit for Boss Doggs and for myself.

Business kept growing and at first everyone was surprised.

That spot was the worst of the three. But it was only the worst because the people that had previously been in that spot treated it as the worst. I went in with an open mind, a positive attitude, and a belief that I could increase sales by my personality and the great product.

And I did all year.

My first year running a hot dog cart on OSU campus was in the books. I had a spectacular year, made a ton of money for a college student, had a ball doing it, and stayed on the hot dog cart gig all summer long, with Eric inviting me back for another year running my own cart at the end of it.

My second year running the cart coincided with my junior year in college. It was very interesting that as I began taking my core business and marketing classes to compare what they told me in the classroom and the lecture hall with what I was seeing on a daily basis from my own sales job out in the field. The points I was being told in the classroom didn't always necessarily ring true at the hot dog stand, but only someone with real world work experience would know that at the time of the class. Most of the other students didn't know if something did or did not ring true in the real world because they hadn't had a chance to experience that real life work experience quite yet.

I can honestly say I had some great professors at Ohio State and the Fisher College of Business continues to be one of the best education centers in the country.

But I learned more about sales and business from the hot dog stand than I did in the classroom.

The hot dog stand taught me about customer service. Everyone preaches about customer service. You see mission statements every single day that say "We put our customers first" or "Customer service is priority number one."

Well, yeah, it should be. If it wasn't, we might have a crisis on our hands.

But the hot dog stand taught me you need to go beyond just treating customers well. You need to treat them like royalty and be absolutely the most remarkable, memorable, and beneficial person in the world to them.

Being REMARKABLE is what increases your sales.

Being MEMORABLE will create long-term partnerships.

Being BENEFICIAL makes people want to not just be friends with you but to do business with you.

That is what the hot dog stand taught me. And that is something you cannot learn from a marketing textbook in college.

It also taught me the inner workings, positives, and tough times of running a small business.

It gave me an up close and personal look at management of inventory, budget expectations, profitability and margins, revenues, etc.

Boss Doggs was a walking case study for me in a business, the job of sales, and the overall lifestyle of a entrepreneur.

When I would push that hot dog cart out every morning – we loaded our carts up from 7:00 a.m. to 8:00 a.m., then drove around in the official Boss Doggs van, dropped coolers off, and came back to push the cart about a mile to each of our respective locations – I was thinking about how I was going to WOW my customers that day.

I had in my head the numbers that I needed to hit in order to make a certain amount of commission. I started cooking the regulars' orders that needed to be ready in a minimal amount of time each day to ensure their happiness and repeat business.

Boss Doggs, or anything like it, was not taught in my business management or marketing books. We learned about how you needed the 4 P's of marketing (product, place, price, promotion) and the ways in which companies like Wal-Mart and Merck executed these P's on a national and global level.

What we learned in the classroom was interesting and to a certain degree beneficial. But it didn't provide the necessary lessons or framework that our generation needed in order to be prepared when stepping into the job market. We were fast-tracking head-on into a recession and as students we were learning platforms and programs we could talk about in interviews. But we had no idea what it would be like when it was applied to our jobs and we were told to hit the ground running.

Hot dogs gave me that missing perspective. Hot dogs gave me an edge. All day long my friends thought I was just hanging out selling meat off a grill.

I was.

But I was doing so much more than that. I was learning how to become a sales and marketing specialist and what a small business needed to not only survive but thrive and flourish.

On top of everything Eric taught me about attitude and customer service, what I learned from running my own cart for three years was experience that can't be replicated inside of a classroom or in the tiny print of a textbook.

I worked at Boss Doggs through the end of my senior year. It was one of the most gratifying and fun experiences of my life. But most importantly it was a framework for my future. It showed me that it was much more about being yourself and being passionate and wanting to WOW your customers than it was about making sure you had the proper media mix when going after your target market.

Boss Doggs paid for my college in full without me having to take out loans. It also paid for some great spring breaks to Daytona Beach, the Bahamas, and Jamaica! I'll leave those stories for the campfire and the water cooler, though.

Boss Doggs paid me forward in business and sales experience at least an extra decade in terms of value, and for that I will always be grateful. Eric ran a great business there, and I still keep in touch with him today. While he decided to eventually leave the business, I am sure he has great memories of running it for well beyond just my reign there as one of his employees.

Carry Out

1) You determine how your day will go the second you get out of bed.

2) Customer service is universal. It doesn't matter the industry, treat your customers like royalty if you want to have a chance to succeed.

Chapter 5: REFRIED BEANS

Ahem! "Michael Rudd." "Michael, great to meet you, we are looking forward to having this conversation with you today."

Ah, the interview process at the Fisher College of Business for internships my junior year.

Flash backward a bit. I was working the hot dog cart, going to class full time at night, hitting the gym six days a week, and maintaining an active college student lifestyle meaning I was frequently hitting the local watering holes multiple times a week. And I was beginning the process of interviewing for a summer internship between my junior and senior years.

Fisher College of Business does a stand-up job of getting great companies with big names and wonderful opportunities onto the OSU campus to interview students' right there so you don't have to go travel all over the state or country to do so on your own dime.

It is simply outstanding what they offer at the Fisher College of Business to help line you up with interviews. I interviewed with Scotts Company (where I actually did a fun, laid-back sales internship during my senior year), Phillip Morris, Aldi, P&G, etc. Cardinal Health and GE were there too, and the list could go on forever.

There was an online system where you could submit your resume and cover letter to request an interview with these companies for internships and for full time jobs, if so desired, and if they wanted to speak with you, they would schedule a time. It was a streamlined and painless process, and I set up as many interviews as I could with these companies.

I was in the midst of my hot dog work, though, and I was learning one very important attribute of what you want in your job.

A LOT OF FUN.

If anyone reads my blog or has been to the website, you will know that at MarketingFunWithMike I always preach about passion and working a job that you love. If your heart is not in it, then you aren't in it. Believe it or not, there are millions of people on this earth who bypass extra money for a lot of fun at their job. I would do so in a heartbeat.

Fortunately, Boss Doggs both paid me well and gave me the opportunity for A LOT OF FUN.

As I began the internship interview process, I had one thing clearly in mind. I wasn't going to work an internship at a company that I wasn't passionate about and do a job that I didn't find to be a lot of fun.

Well . . .

These companies were all wonderful in terms of revenue, profitability, evolving on global scales, outstanding benefits, excellent and nice people, etc. But I was having trouble saying to myself that being a "Territory Sales Intern" or a "Brand Marketing Intern" for companies I knew little about until I began to research them for my interview – and did not have much passion for their products once I did – was a such a great idea.

Now, none of these companies were bad, and the internship opportunities were outstanding. But my goals were to be passionate and have a lot of fun.

These opportunities were not "it."

And I knew they weren't going to be "it" for my life. Not the life I wanted to continue to lead. I was trying to become a remarkable employee at an organization that wanted to use my enthusiasm and my marketing and hot dog background in a fun and productive way.

I decided to scratch what I was doing partway through the process and instead focus on finding a company I truly wanted to work for. And "just to have an internship" is not a good reason to work somewhere.

This is advice I still offer today and really came from these interviews for internships. Because before that, I never had to work somewhere I didn't want to work. Up to that point at the age of 19, I had only worked at a hot dog stand, a golf course with all of my buddies, and a retirement home as a server with a ton of friends and neighborhood kids.

Toeing the company line had not been in my vocabulary yet.

And it wasn't going to start now.

Don't let it ever start for you. Everyone in this world has special abilities and something they are truly great at. There are plenty of people who love working for big companies and are truly passionate about doing what I did not want to do. Don't ever be discouraged and don't ever settle for anything other than what is the best and the happiest solution for you.

If you make a goal to have a career with A LOT OF FUN you will. You will create ART each day instead of CLOCKING IN.

You will display passion instead of somberness.

When you walk into the office, you will say, "What an incredible day, Joe" instead of "Not bad for a Monday, I guess, Joe."

Hot Dogs and A Lot of Fun were starting to teach me more about what I wanted to spend my life doing than I ever thought possible.

The need for an internship still existed and how many companies in Columbus were ones that fit my list of heavy expectations?

There was still one thing missing that I didn't know I needed yet: "A Little Marketing."

Thank the Lord above for letting that awesome independent radio station's signal tune in at the hot dog storage area each morning my last two years. Because one morning, thinking about what I wanted to go after now that I'd scrapped my big corporate territory intern gigs, there was a radio station guy talking like he was having the best day of his life.
He was talking like this even though it was 10 degrees and snowing on a February Monday in Ohio. His enthusiasm for the job couldn't be hidden.

CD101: The Alternative Station. OF COURSE! It was my favorite radio station in the city.

Passion for it: Check.

Positivity: Check.

A local station that cared about its customers so deeply that they truly tried to be remarkable every day: Check.

An internship that would add more marketing and promotional experience to my resume and teach me about a new industry to help when I entered the full-time job market in a year: Check.

I wanted them.

I guess I had to see if they wanted me.

Carry Out

1) Find an internship and experience that is fun and makes your mind work.

2) CD101 is now CD 102.5 in Columbus on the radio dial and still ROCKS THE HOUSE.

Chapter 6: GREEN OLIVES

CD101 exemplified the type of company I wanted to work for. It was, and still is, a locally owned and operated radio station. It was very popular among my age demographic and conveyed an attitude that they were more concerned about their listeners (aka their core customers) than pleasing a board of directors. I am thankful to this day for my year-and-a-half-long internship at CD101.

After a series of interviews, I was hired there for my marketing and promotions internship the summer before my senior year, and it wound up being an internship I would stay at throughout my final year of college.

It is a family over there, and they taught me how to take care of your customers and be even more remarkable than I thought I was already being.

Karac was promotions director at CD101 at the time. He and station general manager Randy (who still runs the show over there; both of them own two of the most unstoppable motors I have ever seen) were the ones who hired me. To this day I consider Karac one of the strongest influences on my career and one of the best mentors I ever hard. The man is an absolute machine when it comes to focus, dedication, execution, and follow-through, and we worked on and set up more turnkey marketing plans and promotions for clients than I have words or time to describe.

My favorite work there was when we monitored a few of the Top 40 stations in the market. CD101 had the most extended playlist and variety of songs probably in the state. It was amazing to me to realize listening to Top 40 stations how often their songs are repeated in a week. I know that is their gimmick, but it was something that really opened my eyes. The promos we churned out in the studio, like "CD101: The station that promises it won't spin Nickelback 648 times in a week," were 100% true. When a Top 40 station has a hit song in rotation, it is crazy how many times it gets spun in just the time span of a week! Good for Nickelback. Tough cookies for me, I guess!

Karac is in New York these days, and I'd put money on it that he will one day be the Ari Gold of the music agency business. Without all of the anger and emotional issues Ari had in "Entourage."

We launched campaigns that mattered, that enabled clients to see their return on investment with the radio station.

All of the lessons and stories I read about in my marketing books were finally being put forth into life for me. It was no longer about memorizing definitions and re-reading chapters. It was about implementation and achieving success.

Randy still works there and runs the station, and I also credit and thank him for the drive that he showed me; he set a great example of the nonstop motor you must have to succeed in the music and the media industry. One of the reasons I think I have been able to sustain longer term relationships and partnerships with clients in an industry known for short-selling and under-servicing was Randy and the sales and promotions and on-air team he had at the station when I worked there.

We needed the clients as much as they needed us, and we made sure they were win-win partnerships. If you can't secure two-way partnerships and one side feels the slightest bit taken advantage of, then it can never develop into the long-term level-five top-of-the-line relationship you need to truly make success.

We were a small independent radio station going against the big "high and mighty Clear Channel"; but we had intangibles they didn't have. We had compassion, we had empathy, we had attitude, and to quote MIA, "Nobody on the corner had swagga like us." We were ourselves.

As I worked at Boss Doggs and at CD101 my final year of college, I was able to come into my own and know that you don't make it far by sucking up and not voicing your opinion or thoughts.

These two companies taught me that to truly make it in this world and the sales industry, the most important things you need are your honor and to know yourself. It may have taken me a little bit to figure this out and I had some difficulties in finding it but CD101 knew who it was then, they know who they are now, and they will never apologize for it. That laid the groundwork for me and once I found that I have never given it up and will never give who I am or my honor up for anything ever again.

In sales I often hear how important it is not to show your emotions and to guard against letting your true feelings and excitement come through to a client initially.

I say B O G U S.

Being myself was what helped hyper-accelerate my focus, my energy, and my attitude. I wasn't trying to be somebody I wasn't and it showed when I started working with clients on site at promotions and working on marketing strategy in the CD101 studio. They gave me that freedom to be myself, and that is something that is not always given in a corporate environment.

I always tell my clients now that "I am who I am when I am sitting here with you, out with my family and friends, talking to strangers, or speaking to my boss. I will show you my true self all the time."

Do that in sales and, quite honestly, in any job or relationship, it will shine through to people. I really think if we were all our true happy selves everyday, you would see a lot less honking in traffic, more people waving at strangers when walking down the street, and more smiles on your co-workers' faces.

People are naturally happy. Remember back to when you were a kid, and think about how much fun you had every day. I read the other that the average child smiles 2,000 times a day and the average adult smiles 14 times a day!

14?!?!?!?!

What a depressing stat! But it proves that happiness is within all of us. Unfortunately, somewhere along the line we start getting caught up in the minutiae of life and feeling bogged down into a long daily checklist.

We stop being ourselves and we stop smiling. When we stop smiling, we stop loving what we do for a career. When we stop loving what we do, we stop taking care of our customers. We stop taking care of our customers and we eventually start losing customers. We start losing customers and we lose our job or our business.

Be happy. Be a kid. Be yourself. Smile and laugh often. You would be amazed how much I apply this to my everyday life and working with my clients and how much it helps all of our moods and our conversations.

So, CD101 gave me my little bit of marketing experience (okay, a ton of it) that I needed to couple with my takeaways and the knowledge I'd gained at the hot dog stand and at the Ohio State University. I was leaving college with no debt, I had a blast, I graduated with a double major on time, and I had two incredible job experiences that really energized the personal and business sides of my life.

Now I just needed to figure out what on earth I was going to do with all of this knowledge I had supposedly gained in hot dogs, independent radio, textbook studying, and taking care of customers.

Radio sales seemed like it would be a good fit.

A side note about smiling. I think it would be hysterical (yes, those were my words) to get a tattoo on my chest or shoulder of one of those yellow smiley faces with black eyes that says "Smile Often."

The wife does not necessarily agree.

Carry Out

1) The customer is the kingpin always.

2) Enjoyment at the job is the key to becoming great.

Chapter 7: FRITOS

The problem about radio sales at the time I wanted to enter the field, as I quickly figured out, was that no one was hiring.

People enjoy selling radio and working at a radio station. You are out and about all day and not stuck at a desk eight hours a day. You get to work with local businesses day in and day out and have a feeling of pride in the community when you help them out. DJs are out-of-their-minds weird, funny, and entertaining to be around.

Needless to say, almost every radio station in town was looking for someone with two to three years prior media sales experience.

CD101 did not have an opening. And they were so small that an opening was unlikely to come up even in a year or two. So, sadly I knew I would part ways with them when my graduation came upon us.

But there was one station in town, in fact, one of the cooler and highly ranked stations as the heritage classic rock station in the market, looking for new people. So I went in for an interview with Mitchell and Ross. I found out later that Mitchell and Ross probably had no interest in hiring me for anything other than selling the classic rock station's little sister, a hard rock station that had the lowest ratings in the market.

But something incredible happened in my two interviews with them. Actually I should say there was nothing magical about it at all! I honestly just acted like myself and didn't fake anything. Some would categorize that as magic or luck, I say the norm if you are yourself.

I smiled, I was myself, and I told them about my radio station experience at CD101 and how I was just finishing up putting myself through college by selling hot dogs.

I went into extreme detail when they asked me about the hot dog stand, and I must have impressed them, because they hired me at the ripe age of 21, just a few days before my birthday and a month or two before my graduation date! I would start the week after I graduated.

It really felt like time sped by during my final two months of college, I had a job lined up and ready to go when I graduated so it was a pretty relaxing time. I had fun with my friends, worked hard at Boss Doggs and at CD101 and finished all my final classes up, until it was time to bid goodbye to them and Ohio State (well, I still lived on campus and was one of maybe five out of 30 friends who graduated in four years, so this was not a brave new world. We were all still enjoying the college lifestyle whether we had finished school or not.)

Once again, thank you, Eric, Randy, Karac, my professors and everyone else at those places who taught me so much. We had so much fun together during those years. My brother would be keeping the hot dog legacy alive, though, by continuing to work with Eric at Boss Doggs. But that is for another book. Maybe we'll co author a book called "Two Brothers Slanging Street Meat."

Moving ahead.

The feeling you get your first day on a job. There is nothing people find more uncomfortable than the first day at a new place. If you couple that with your first day in real-life American working conditions, you have a perfect storm. I was actually so nervous that day I left my packed lunch at the kitchen table, only to get a phone call from my girlfriend Katie when I was four blocks down the road to get back over there if I wanted to eat my first day on the job! There were businesspeople all around me acting very professional, co-workers talking in a radio lingo I didn't understand, plus everyone seemed so much older (maybe because they were and still are at times).

I was trying to just wrap my head around what I was supposed to be doing. Training kits, sales videos, etc. were thrown on my desk and I was told to get to work.

It went on like this for a few weeks. I would go on a few sales calls here and there with some of the more seasoned reps at the radio station. (Side note: Not even my future wife, who I met there, offered much assistance those first few weeks – haha!)

Everything I had just pushed myself through in terms of being myself and having fun was out the window.

I was at a standstill. I had no accounts and a three-month salary of $2K per month. After that, I would either be on 100% commission or most likely fired.

Being fired seemed to be the direction.

I didn't know how it happened. Everything had been going so well. But I made a mistake those first few weeks. Maybe you could blame it on nerves, or being in a new environment, but I take blame in one place only and that is on me. I got away from the core traits that got me there in the first place. I got away from what Ross and Mitchell saw in me and what Karac and Eric and my professors had seen in me.

At about the start of week four, Ross called me into his office. He told me he liked what I had been doing so far. I told him I wasn't doing anything but going on sales calls with other reps, watching dumb sales training videos, and learning the demographics of our radio station.

Ross saw that I was frustrated and put together what he later told me was something he thought I had no chance in hell of even getting a meeting with someone for. He did think it would show him how much hustle I had inside of myself. He called it the "Best Bartender" package and told me to take it to every restaurant and bar in the city that wasn't already being called on by our station and try to sell them the idea for an on-site event with the radio station.

This is where I got my mojo back. It clicked. I was out selling hot dogs and smiling again. I was having fun, cold calling, walking into businesses, setting up meetings. I went wild.

And you know why? I went back to what got me there in the first place.

I tried to change once I landed there into some uptight trained and professional account manager. Why was I trying to be so serious? I was selling Led Zeppelin, Pink Floyd, and a morning show that was so good and so raunchy at times that they could sell themselves just by mentioning their name.

As my sales career or, more specifically, my media sales career has evolved, I find it interesting to look back at the way you sell as an individual in the industry.

As recently as the year 2000, radio sales were based on rates. You had to negotiate with clients and advertising agencies as to how much you were willing to sell a commercial for and often an agency would send you back over an order. Sometimes for $5K for a week, but sometimes for $200K for a year!

Sounds easy, doesn't it?

Well, I won't say it was easy, because there were relationships being built then, and old-school sales cold-calling out of a phone book was about as difficult as it can get. But it wasn't exactly rocket science. Apparently, this got flipped upside down while I was in college, and by the time I arrived at the classic rock station in mid-2005 you couldn't just give somebody rates.

You had to build them an "idea." Nowadays I will go into much more detail and customization, but the Best Bartender Package for me was the start of "idea selling."

Although I did not wind up selling this particular package, it gave me the chance to get back to what I had done to get myself there, and it reminded me that this job would be no different from what I had done before. Be myself, super-serve those customers, add some marketing sense, have a lot of fun, and I would be able to make it.

Ironically, selling zero "Best Bartender Packages" sold put me back on track.

Soon I was meeting with those same bars and restaurants and working on much more customized ideas and we eventually got to work together.

My first sale finally came seven weeks into the job. It was faster than most, but not atypical for a first sale in terms of how long it took a rookie to achieve.

It was a local chain of adult magazines, DVD's, and "toys." What a memorable way to officially start my radio sales career. I remember trying to play it cool and low key and Ross made me stand up and give him a big high five and everyone congratulated me on selling a bunch of "porn."

My batting average was no longer zero and I was ready to go!

All because I stopped focusing on being a great seller, negotiator, numbers-of-your-station guy and went back to zeroing in on ideas, the client's needs, smiling, and having a good time doing it.

When we enter a job, at no matter what age or level, too often we think we need to become that job. I think that is incorrect. We need to let the job mold around us. We need to give it our own twist. Because there is nothing worse, especially in sales or marketing, than somebody trying to force something they aren't on people.

People are smart and have an innate sense for that. Don't ever try to force an unnatural personality on someone. It won't work. Your clients won't buy it because they don't buy who you are trying to be.

Ross, I thank you for giving me the unsellable Best Bartender Package. If it wasn't for that idea you made up on a whim to get me out of the office that day, things could have turned out differently.

Onward and forward I went. Sales and marketing was evolving at a rapid rate and we had a lot of objections, concerns, and hills to climb if radio was going to survive in a culture full of Facebook, MySpace (yes, in 2005 and 2006 it was MySpace, not Twitter), iPods, and satellite radio.

How was it going to be possible to sell our old friend radio when so many new products looked so much shinier and more fun to play with to our clients?

Carry Out

1) 100% commission is no joke. It is tough not knowing what you will make next month.

2) Don't sit around and wait for stuff to happen at a new job. Go get it or you will be out the door faster than you can count to ten.

Chapter 8: GREEN CHILES

Sales stories you just can't make up!
Story #1

Sprinkled into this book will be chapters of true stories (with names of people changed at times) about real life encounters throughout my career that are exactly what the title says: Sales stories you just can't make up! It is a little glimpse into the random day to day interactions with a sales person and their prospects and clients.

Onto story numero UNO!

Ross comes onto the overhead speaker that can be heard throughout the entire radio station: "I have a big announcement and congrats to give out. One of our sales people had a great day out there and closed a great account. I would like to congratulate Mike Rudd on closing POOP BASKET DOT COM."

Now, that is not exactly the name and the company no longer exists. But, yes, I had met with a guy the previous day with a website business where you could order a gag gift of rubber fake poop and he would ship it to someone's house or business in a nice gift basket with a bow and when you opened it up . . . well you get it. SURPRISE!

He had a very small budget (I think it was honestly like $250 on the small active rock station that we had there) and he did sell quite a few initially from the website, but he never got the business to where he could make a living from it and eventually had to shut it down.

The reason I tell this story is little did I know that my future wife and current co-worker, who at the time I didn't really even talk to much yet, had sold about $85,000 worth of business that day. When Ross got on the intercom, she thought for sure it was to congratulate her.

Nope.

Sorry, honey, but my $250 worth of poop baskets happened to be far more interesting than your multiple annual contracts with insurance companies and auto dealers.

To say I stole her thunder that day would be an understatement.

Carry Out

1) Amazingly she still married me.

Chapter 9: BAKED BEANS

Sales can be done many different ways and by many different types of people. But as I began to get into the groove at my job, I realized there were a few keys to what I did that really enabled me to put myself and my clients in the best situation to win no matter what outside factors were involved.

Over the next few chapters I will begin to lay the groundwork for how to keep you – and, most importantly, your clients – on the winning end as we move through the digital age. Keep in mind that when I entered this industry the digital age had not begun to go into full swing. That's why I feel these traits will outlast this era and go into the next age, so long as we continue to enhance, moderate, and improve the core traits that go around them.

The most important thing you can do every day goes back to hot dogs for me. And that was putting the customer on the highest level. Not just trying to be good at customer service, but super-serving that client to such a degree they would not consider ever severing your relationship.

Think for a moment about companies that list customer service as an important part of their mission statement but in reality are at about a 5 on a scale of 1 to 10 in customer service.

Then consider those local businesses that remember your name each time you come in, neighborhood companies like Joe's Hardware that go to such a high degree of effort to take care of you that they rate an 8 on customer service.

To succeed in 100% commission sales in the coming years you need to be at a 10!

That's right, a 10 and you will constantly be striving for higher!

At the hot dog stand I realized customer service was the one thing I had the most control of. The weather changed sometimes, kids ran out of money at the end of each quarter a lot, and we would run out of a product from time to time.

The one core competency that I could always have in my back pocket if I so choose to use it was being a 10!

What does it take to be a 10?

The standards still apply. You need to be on time for your meetings, write thank-you cards after each step in the process, come in with great thought-provoking ideas, the best price you can fairly offer, etc.

But then you need to go beyond the mission-statement level into what I like to refer to as the "Zappos Level." To find out how great Zappos.com is at customer service I suggest you read Tony Hseih's (the CEO of Zappos) wonderful book called "Delivering Happiness."

If there is one thing Zappos prides itself on it is customer service. The last time I was in Las Vegas I wanted to take a tour of their headquarters, but unfortunately I had a limited amount of time and they had a few huge tours booking up huge chunks of their day. The lady I spoke with, just another outstanding customer service rep, offered to come in early – hours before the office was open – on her day off and give myself and my wife our own private tour.

We never said we were customers, fans of the book or of their culture, nothing.

That is why Zappos has its own level of customer service, the gold standard. If you are at the Zappos level, you are in the 99th percentile!

But with everything changing on the digital and global landscape, I want to encourage everyone to reach for the "REMARKABLE" level.

The remarkable level is a trait that we can bring to our careers every single day and that no one can ever take from us. The only person who can rob us of it is ourselves.

The REMARKABLE level is my own new standard that I wish to reach, retain, and improve on every day. I don't get there every day; in fact, many days I probably don't reach it. But when I do I am in the zone and I am offering my clients a level of customer service that no one else in the market can offer.

And I learned the REMARKABLE level at the hot dog stand, I improved on it while I was at the classic rock station, and I still work on it every day.

The REMARKABLE level thinking started for me after I sold the Poop Guy on our active rock station.

As I said, he was struggling with his business and maybe in the grand scheme of things it was not meant to be. But I liked the guy and while it was worth only about $50 in commission, I did everything in my power to help him get the results he needed. In hindsight he didn't have enough money to spend to get the word out, and social media was not anywhere near where it is today in terms of spreading a message.

But I gave him extra on-air spots, voiced the promos for him, leased out an extra copy writer to help me, and even negotiated his product into some on-air giveaways because I really wanted to see him succeed.

When our campaign was said and done and he was struggling with going on with his business, I told him how sorry I was that I couldn't have done more. He told me that I was the least of his problems and without me he wouldn't have come close to where he had gotten thus far.

That struck a chord with me.

I wanted to be so important to my clients that they couldn't imagine not having me around to help them out on a day-to-day basis. We were not only giving them a great product at a reasonable price that was making them a profit but I was so necessary to their daily dealings that the thought of being without me would be devastating.

Look, every single year I lose clients for whom I think I do remarkable things. Then I keep clients every single year with whom I think I need to improve my service. But I have learned from hot dogs that being REMARKABLE is one thing you can have under your control, when all the other factors in your day are "variables." All other things aside, you can hang your hat at going past the mission-statement level, going past the Tony Hsieh and Zappos level, and reaching the REMARKABLE level!

I learned from my fake poop client that being remarkable means performing at such a high level that business on a daily basis without your services and help would be unbearable.

There I was at a classic rock station, a rookie who had been given no accounts, was the least senior member on the staff, and still knew very little about the world of radio sales. But I knew I could make it. I knew in my heart that I had something that if I brought it with me every day, I could beat the odds, gain and retain clients, and slowly climb up the ladder at a radio station typically reserved for senior members of media sales in the prime of their careers and in their mid-40s.

I was 23, hungry, and maybe delusional. But I knew I could be the highest biller on that staff within a year or two and not only survive but thrive. My first step, and a step I still have listed to make sure I do it every day now, is to be REMARKABLE.

If you stop reading this book after this chapter, remember to do this every day and you will always have a fighting chance in your favor in the world of sales, marketing, being a business owner and any other career path that gives you the freedom to be REMARKABLE.

Carry Out

1) Be remarkable.

2) If you think you are remarkable, strive for more.

Chapter 10: SPICY MUSTARD

Sales stories you just can't make up!
Story #2

The general manager of a local gentlemen's club kept telling me. "The reason I am not spending more money with you is your radio station used to let the dancers and the feature [the traveling adult film star who was in for the weekend was typically the feature] come in and do an interview on the morning show on Fridays. It was great exposure, a lot of fun, and one of the main reasons I used to spend the money I did with your station. If you can get the interviews back on the air, I will start spending that type of money again."

I was almost through my second year at the classic rock station, and by this point I had accumulated through new business, attrition, and a lot of cold calling a decent list that I was continuing to grow.

One of the rewards for my early successes was that about a year or so into the job I received most of the gentlemen's club business in the area when the rep who used to have the accounts moved onto a new job. We were a classic rock station (think middle-aged men as our core listeners) so it was big business.

What I felt was the biggest possible club for growth on my list kept throwing me this same objection. It didn't matter that I was trying to be remarkable, it didn't matter that I was trying to be fun and myself around him. The bottom line was this club used to get a free interview on our highly rated morning show and it was not happening anymore. Nothing in my power could get them to spend more money unless I could get the interviews done.

Months passed and the billing would decrease even more. I begged our manager to reconsider, but he told me it was a corporate thing (we were owned by a large national radio company) and his hands were tied.

Until one day we were sold.

We were sold to a small radio company. The owner and his right-hand man – I'll call them Jason and Leonard in this story – were in town from the get-go and wanted to go on sales calls and meet all of our clients.

Leonard told me he specifically wanted to see any clients we had issues with because of the former big-company owner. I told him about this gentlemen's club, and he said there'd be no problem getting those interviews back; let's just get them to commit to a year's worth of advertising at the level they used to spend at.

Sounded to me like a fair deal and a great plan the client would go for.

On a Tuesday night about ten days after the new company took over our classic rock station, I picked up Leonard from his downtown hotel and we rolled out to the suburbs to meet with the club.

This was my life now: sales meetings at the gentlemen's clubs on a Tuesday night. It was pretty unusual stuff, but entertaining for a 24-year-old, to say the least.

Leonard and I met with the club's GM and came to the solid agreement with a handshake that they would get a morning show interview once a month and be on the afternoon show three times a month.

He was happy. We were happy. It was a win-win partnership.

Leonard had this knack for wanting to get the client to sign right there on the spot.

One thing I'd learned with working with the gentlemen's clubs was that their word was way more solid than even an official order you would receive from an advertising agency. If they committed to it, they weren't going to cancel it.

Leonard LOVES sales calls. No, wait. Let me rephrase that. Leonard is OBSESSED with sales calls! The man lives for the sales call.

Leonard kindly asked the general manager if he would sign the contract, the general manager said, "What contract?"

Leonard replied, "This contract, man!"

Leonard had written down the weekly dollar amount he had committed to, what he would receive in commercials each week, and the totals for the year for him.

What did he write it down on???

A cocktail napkin with a big fat logo of the club on the middle of it!

The general manager double-checked that Leonard was serious (Leonard was very serious), signed it, and ordered the three of us shots of tequila.

We toasted and after another drink or so, Leonard and I left.

Leonard was like a kid in the candy store with that cocktail napkin. I think he wanted me to get it framed. I made a copy of it and emailed it to the general manager to remind him (in case it was a hazy night) that he had committed to the new program.

That was my first and only signed contract on a cocktail napkin at a gentlemen's club.

But Leonard taught me something that night.

It wasn't about the razzle or the dazzle. Pretty presentations meant nothing. All the client cared about was how you would help his or her business.

If the proposal was written on a cocktail napkin while Leonard was using the restroom, so be it, if it was outstanding.

The only razzle and dazzle clients care about is RESULTS!

Carry Out

1) If you have a sales bucket list, having a client sign an order on a cocktail napkin should be on it.

2) You are only valuable to the client if you continue to under-promise and over-deliver. Not the other way around.

Chapter 11: RELISH

We have to be remarkable to be able to stay in the sales and marketing business and stay on top of it.

But what else does one have to do?

The second point or trait that has helped me and will continue to help me is something I learned from hot dogs and is why I wound up at CD101 and the classic rock station.

If you don't like it, don't sell it!

If you aren't passionate about the product yourself, I don't think you should represent it.

Now you have read and will probably read and hear from many people that it doesn't matter if you like or use the product that you represent. As long as you know the target market and who you can help, it is okay to sell it.

I say NO!

I say NO if you want to be extraordinary at what you do and not just an average sales person or marketing specialist or business owner.

If you want to go through each year scraping by and being scared of losing your job, then it is okay to represent a product you don't love.

But if you want to turn your job into a career, crush those budgets, and take your game to another level, be passionate about your product!

When I decided to try to work at CD101, it was simple. I loved the station and thought it would be a job I would like.

When I chose to pursue opportunities at the classic rock station and the sports talk station where I am now, I did it because I enjoy classic rock music and sports!

It helps you have conversations with your clients when they ask you about your product. You sound more into it and excited about what you are representing.

Too many times in my career I have worked with people who don't have an interest in the world of using or listening to or watching the product that they represent, and 95% of the time it prevents them from truly achieving greatness.

No matter how good a salesperson they are, how in-depth and cutting-edge their marketing plan is, how wonderful a negotiator they are, if they don't really like the product, it shows through eventually.

Never work at a job you don't like or in a career that you wouldn't want to lay it all on the line for.

During my senior year of college I picked up an additional internship with a local recruitment company here in Columbus. It was just 10 hours a week, 2 five-hour shifts during weekdays. I thought it would be a good resume enhancer (which it was) and provide a peek into an industry that I didn't know much about (which it did.)

The guy who hired me and everyone on the staff there were great people, and I thank them to this day for the opportunity.

But I did not care for IT recruiting and consulting, and I loathed having to go in there every day!

I couldn't stand it, in fact. It was only 8 weeks long, 10 hours a week. It was only a grand total of two 40-hour work weeks! But I couldn't get out of there quick enough. When the internship was up there was an opportunity to renew and they wanted me to come back for another eight weeks. I felt bad because, like I said, they were all good people and I learned quite a bit. But the most important takeaway I had from that internship was: "NEVER WORK A JOB YOU DON'T LIKE!" Not for money, not for fame, not for a stepping stone to another gig. Just say NO!

That was the last time I did, and I don't plan on doing it again in my life.

If you want to reach the pinnacle of your industry, be the top sales rep in the state, and eventually the country in your career path, please write down a list of what you truly are passionate about and love to do and find a job within that industry.

Another good reason to join a field that you are into is you are knowledgeable about it already! You know it inside and out and as you continue to learn about it, you will enjoy the research and the reading.

It all goes back to doing what you truly love and enjoy. I knew selling hot dogs, classic rock, and Ohio State sports would all be fun. So I chose to sell them instead of insurance, cigarettes, lawn care, or financial services.

But if those interest you instead, by all means go find that passion and that job that you love and start selling and marketing the heck out of it!

Carry Out

1) Represent a product you yourself love and are passionate about.

2) Never work at a job you don't like unless it means your children or significant other won't eat or have a roof over their heads.

Chapter 12: JALAPENOS

Sales stories you just can't make up!
Story #3

It was just one of those days at the hot dog stand. It was fall quarter of senior year and the weather was beautiful.

Business had been great since I got the food cooked up at 10:15 a.m., and I had at least five people in line until 3:20 p.m. or so.

Clean-up and push-out time back to the Ohio Union for inventory and budget counts was usually 3:30 p.m., and the last hour was typically slow. So by about 2:45 p.m. or so, you stopped adding more food to cook and instead focused on keeping everything warm.

Well, being so busy, I had just lost track of time, and at 3:20 p.m. when I finally had my first breath not behind the hot dog grill with a huge line since 10:15 a.m. I realized I had a ton of food left.

Not more than two minutes later the class bell rang and the line was back. It was order after order after order.

Finally at about 3:40 p.m. I had finished up, or so I thought.

I was out of chicken, out of drinks, out of chips, out of brats, you get the picture.

But I still had six hot dogs and two Bahama Mama (think spicy brats) sausages left. A group of college kids came up and said they would ransack what I still had in my cart.

Great! Being an efficient person, I always loved having a cart empty of meat at the end of the day because then no food was thrown out when we got back. But it was hard to manage and predict.

CRAP! I suddenly realized I was also out of hot dog buns.

I apologized and said to come back the next day and grab some on the house (be remarkable), but those college kids said no worries. Give them the hot dogs plain, no bun they told me.

Okay, I guess I could see placing the plain naked hot dog or Bahama Mama in their hands in a napkin.

Nope, out of napkins too!

And they wanted condiments as well, they proclaimed.

I proceeded to place the Bahama Mama's and hot dogs in the palms of their hands where we threw some onions on top and ketchup or mustard along the meat. To say the least believers in good table manners would have thrown a fit!

A cool beverage to wash it down?

Chunks of ice from my empty drink cooler.

I was in shock. Only in college. They wiped the leftover mustard, hot dog grease, and water on their pants.

They paid me, thanked me, tipped me, and I thanked them.

What a fun, gross, strange sale at the end of the biggest day in my personal history of running a hot dog cart!

I sold over $1,600.00 of food and drinks that day. Not to mention almost $100.00 in tips before my commission. If I could have made that every day, it would not have been necessary to graduate from college or do anything else in my life. The hot dog cart would have made me richer than I ever cared to be.

So, yes, you can serve someone hot dogs, mustard, and onions into the palm of their hand, give them ice cubes to wash it down, and have one of the greatest days in your sales career!

And the idea of making $1600.00 worth of sales in five and a half hours should answer anyone's question as to whether not you can make a career out of selling hot dogs.

Carry Out

1) College kids will eat anything, prepared any way, at any time.

Chapter 13: CHILI

Funnels

If you are in any type of sales or marketing job you have heard your manager ask you about how full your funnel is. The sales funnel is how much business you have out there that is pending for a specific amount of time.

There are many different stages of the sales cycle; there is early prospecting and cold calling, followed by meetings that some refer to as the needs-analysis/info-gathering stage, and finally the closing/proposal stages.

The basic idea is that you should have multiple pieces of business in all stages of your funnel.

The fuller you keep your funnel, the better your chances for long-term and sustained success!

Easy, right?

This is probably the most important thing going forward that I and everyone needs to make sure they do if they want to stay in the sales or entrepreneurial industry for any amount of time at the same job.

And it is one of the areas least paid attention to in our jobs.

Hundreds of media reps switch stations across the country every day, smart people see their businesses go under weekly; and great managers and leaders suffer their own job losses because they can't motivate their staffs to take hold and grasp the notion of having a "full funnel."

WHY???

The reason is two-fold. The first reason is people get comfortable. Just like the couple that puts on weight after their first year of marriage, people enjoy getting comfortable.

In sales you need to stay on edge and be uncomfortable at all times in terms of how full you think your funnel is!

Truth be told, it needs to be overflowing and it can never be too full for you to take yourself to the next level.

After my second full year at the classic rock station I had knocked it out of the park compared to my first year. I quadrupled my income and made more money in one year than I had made the first 20 years of my life combined. I was on the fast track to success. My client list was booming, I was coming up with great ideas for local businesses, and they were seeing great results.

Year three started with heightened expectations and budgets, and I was ready to charge into them full speed.

January I barely hit my budget. February I squeaked by. March thru May I missed my budgets but still billed more than I had the previous year. Then by the time June and July began, I was actually billing less than the year before!

What was going on?? I had been at the classic rock station for three full years now and I was starting a decline.

Looking back, it was pretty simple.

I FAILED to keep my funnel full. I was out trying to hit increased budgets by talking to the same clients. I was not prospecting enough people or cold-calling enough. I had grown comfortable with my list, which people do way too often, and I was now paying for it.

I should have known better.
You need to have a full funnel, more prospects, more pitches, more ideas, more networking, and overall just more people to talk to.

Luckily, I had an opportunity in late July to move on from the classic rock station to a sports talk station in Columbus, Ohio. Being an Ohio State graduate, I was elated at the opportunity.

I avoided any pitfalls with my managers and owners at the classic rock station and was gone before my billing started to plateau. It was a learning experience that I am over dramatizing a tad but I would have needed to quickly retool what I was doing there from a prospecting stand point to have a great finish to the year. I did not manage to keep my funnel full enough to achieve double-digit growth year after year after year. It is not easy but I should have known better. I was still hungry I just didn't realize how hungry I needed to be. I like to think I would have come to my senses and realized in order to continue achieving double digit growth for a fourth year in a row I needed more opportunities in my funnel but I was off to my new gig before I had the chance to figure it out.

I believe keeping the funnel full is a two-fold problem, the first being people get comfortable.

That was NOT my issue.

I didn't get lazy or comfortable. I was still making some new calls and prospecting.

The other problem is people fail to grasp just how full they need to keep their funnel – it needs to be overflowing at all times or you will never be able to achieve long-term, sustainable, outstanding performance.

Year to year, even in the worst economic conditions you will receive budgets that are higher than the year before. If you billed $100,000.00 in November of 2010 and you account for 15% normal attrition plus your 15% estimated growth you could have a budget of $115,000.00 the very next November with only $85,000.00 or so that will be coming back.

Wait a minute. With that attrition, it means you need about $30,000 in new business to achieve that number! That is a lot of new business calls you need to make to get $30k in new business for one month.

People can't get their heads around just how much you need in your funnel. You need to be talking to people constantly, pedal to the metal, thinking of ideas 24 hours a day and seven days a week, networking everywhere you go, and then and only then will you have a full funnel.

It is a lot to ask and it is not easy.

I would say it is the downfall of 75% of sales reps over a two to three year period of time. Good sales reps have a great two-year run, then they either get comfortable or underestimate how much they need in their funnel, and they go back to being "average" or "good."

I fell into that category at the classic rock station.

I am now currently working to ensure I don't fall into that category again. I already have been here over a year longer than I was at the classic rock station and there is no end in sight for my tenure or my funnel getting too light, so it is a great start. But I need to harp on myself every day that it doesn't matter how much billing or how many clients I have.

I must go find new ideas for new people, revisit old ones, and then and only then will I fall into that "great" category for five to ten to twenty years.

It is very possible, though, especially now through social media and digital advertising and the capabilities that we have, to have great long term success in 100% commission sales.

If you want to go from good to great, it starts with your funnel. Keep it overflowed at all times. Be yourself. Talk to everyone you can, upturn every rock, and look inside of every crack, because you never know what is under it unless you give it a glance.

Have fun with it too, because if not, you will burn yourself out. Another trait we all need is to not let ourselves get comfortable and to always, always, overestimate just how much we need in our sales funnel.

If you think you have enough, make another five phone calls and try to set up three more meetings for next week.

Carry Out

1) Keeping your sales funnel of opportunities overflowing is your key to success!

2) Never get comfortable or think your funnel is too full.

Chapter 14: SHREDDED CHEESE

Sales stories you just can't make up!
Story #4

This particular tale is not a firsthand account. But it did happen to a guy I used to work with and it is definitely a story that you CANNOT MAKE UP! I asked Jason for permission to use his experience, and he was happy a story as wild as this would finally get the exposure it deserves.

Back to the gentlemen's clubs (I am not trying to pick on them, but they definitely make for the wildest and funniest sales calls I have ever been on.) Jason worked at the station for a long time before I did and left just as I was getting to the classic rock station. Down the road I worked this account under new ownership and had some great success with them, but at the time of this story Jason was working the account. The old ownership of this specific club had a wild stereotypical gentlemen's club manager working the place and he went by the name of Ronny D.

Jason said he had seen Ronny D do some of the craziest and strangest things at the club when he was picking up checks for advertising or meeting with him about promotions. (Yes, we did a lot of promotions there even though we were a predominantly male station with an almost all male on-air staff.) Not sure why we thought sending male DJ's to strip clubs would get the guys more inclined to go to the club. If you are a heterosexual male, you don't go to strip clubs to see your favorite radio DJ, I would venture to guess.

Ronny D was the manager that we all have seen depicted in the movies. Happy as can be one day, a raving lunatic the next. I had the pleasure of working with Ronny D for only a short period of time before the new ownership came in and he was cut loose, but my time with him was a roller coaster ride.

Ronny D would bring the girls from the club into the studio to cut the radio spots. He and the ladies would make all sorts of noises, come up with hilarious drink and dance special announcements in the ads, etc.

Ronny D would spend ten grand with me one month then nothing the next.

I wonder if Ronny D some months was spending his money on "extracurricular activities" outside his marketing budget, but I can't be sure.

Now back to the story, Jason was meeting with Ronny D and Jason brought with him that night Ronny D's new spot on a cassette tape. Yes, in the '90s, before the days of an mp3 that you could forward to a client via email, before the days of even burning onto a CD, Jason had to dub the commercial onto a cassette tape and take it out to the client to make sure he liked it before it aired.

Ronny D was excited that night to hear the new spot, but the tape deck in his office wasn't working. Ronny D suggested they go out to his purple Cadillac or whatever his ridiculous car of choice was that month and listen to it in his car, according to Jason.

Visualize Jason for a moment. Just a normal dorky white guy with a wife and kids living in the Columbus suburbs, sitting in Ronny D's Cadillac listening to a strip club radio commercial on a tape deck over and over on a Tuesday night. Get that picture in your mind before you proceed.

Finally, Ronny D says it's good to go. Just as Jason and Ronny D are getting ready to get out of the car, Ronny D starts flipping out!

Going into convulsions of some sort, almost like a seizure, and he begins howling like a madman!

Jason is freaking the hell out, to say the least.

Ronny D is rocking back and forth and finally starts yelling, "Needle...give me the F&%!NG needle in the glove box."

It turns out, we later learned, that Ronny D is diabetic. And Ronny D had not kept his blood sugar regulated that day.

Ronny D was now having a diabetic seizure with Jason sitting next to him in the car; in the purple Caddy in the parking lot of the strip club.

All in the sales game right??

Jason whips open the glove box and finds a little first aid kit thing and Ronny D quickly nods approval. Jason hands the kit to him and he goes through the process of filling a needle and raising it high in the air . . .(think "Pulp Fiction" when Uma Thurman is overdosing and gets the needle plunged into her heart) . . . and PLUNGES the needle into his thigh.

Ronny D instantly begins to calm down.

As Jason sat there, I wonder who was actually more relieved when the needle when into that thigh and it was clear that Ronny D was going to be okay. He was certainly happy and relieved.

But how would Jason have explained that one to the cops??

"Um, yeah, officer, we were just sitting there listening to the radio ad. No, um, I mean we weren't doing anything illegal. Oh, why are these needles out all over the car? I think he was a diabetic, yeah, that's it!"

Fortunately, disaster was averted on both sides.

Jason could probably write his own book just of stories of his encounters with Ronny D.

Meanwhile, Jason has moved on and is enjoying one of the most illustrious sales careers of anyone I know.

And Ronny D? I don't really know what happened to him.

If I had to guess, I would say he is the manager of a club in Florida or Arizona somewhere off the beaten path, like Bud was in *Kill Bill 2*.

But for now, remember that as a sales rep, duty calls in several different ways. You have to be prepared for anything, quick on your feet, and with a positive attitude that everything is going to work out.

Jason displayed all of those traits that night and may well have saved Ronny D's life.

Congrats, Jason. Ronny D owes you a cocktail.

Carry Out

1) Ronny D would be hard to keep up with if you partied with him.

2) Jason has told me ten more stories like that about Ronny D. Perhaps I'll write another book called "The Chronicles of Ronny D."

Chapter 15: Sauerkraut

I know everyone wants another Ronny D story, but now we must delve back into what is going to keep you going and performing on a high level in commission sales or owning your own business in the coming decades.

Being remarkable, keeping your funnel full, and representing a product that you love are a great start.

But it takes more. What else do we need?

There is an activity that has helped me and I know is going to be around no matter how much technology changes and evolves, information is shared, etc.

And that activity is READING. (A thank you to my wonderful mother, the retired high school English teacher, who instilled reading in me at a young age, I think I owned all 857 Berenstain Bears Books as a little kid.)

Read every day. Read as much as you can. Books, your favorite blogs, and magazines you enjoy, and anything else you can get your hands on.

There are two things I have learned about reading that have helped me be a stronger sales and marketing professional. First and foremost, READ WHAT YOU WANT TO READ.

There are literally hundreds of business books that get published every week. Don't feel that you have to read every single one of them right away or in any particular order. (Except for this one, read this book over and over and tell your friends about it.) If you behave like that, it will become just a daily chore and get you caught up in the rat race of trying to always keep up with the latest thousands of books and blogs that come out weekly.

And the rat race is something that we should never get bogged down into. There are too many wonderful things to enjoy in life every day.

Read what you want to read.

It doesn't matter what type of book it is. Reading helps us get smarter. Read fiction, nonfiction, business books for your industry, autobiographies, murder mysteries.

Mix it up all of the time!

Reading different types of books make us smarter. It makes us use parts of our brain that we don't typically use, and in the end it helps us get better at our jobs and in our careers.

Read at your own pace as well.

I love to fly through a book and dive right into another one most times. But there are times when I like to go much slower because it is harder to digest all of the information in a particular book at such a fast pace.

As I write this I am reading past sermons and speeches from one of the greatest men to ever live, Dr Martin Luther King, Jr., and it is a slow read for me.

I need to take my time. Reread parts. Think about what it all means that he was preaching and speaking about.

Two years ago I would have felt I had to finish it quickly because I needed to dive back into another marketing or sales book.

Now I choose what I want to read and I go in phases. I will read four business books in a row and then not read one for two months. Or vice versa.

I also have about 20 to 30 blogs I store in my Google reader. Most are business, but some are not. I enjoy getting in there once a day to peruse. I don't read every one through and through, but it is a fun daily activity that gives me a different perspective from the book that I am currently reading.

Reading makes us learn new facts and viewpoints every day. It teaches us ways to get better at what we are doing on a daily basis and it gives our brains triggers it wouldn't otherwise encounter.

Reading fiction after nonfiction or vice versa gives us a new light and opinion on certain matters.

Reading blogs we enjoy varies the way our mind works compared to when we read that mystery novel.

All in all, reading makes us better prepared each day we meet with our clients, it gives us fresh perspective and new ideas, new opinions on the way we view life, facts and knowledge we may not have previously known about other generations, and builds our brain to work in ways that it doesn't always function if you don't force it to.

There is no bad book. Read whatever you want and read often from various genres. It will make you more well rounded and help you be yourself more often when out at meetings with clients.

And being yourself makes you a better salesman, marketing director, business owner, accountant, nurse, teacher, fireman, night club owner, or city councilmen!

Bottom Line: Get better tomorrow by starting to read today.

I suggest the best way to get into it if you don't currently read is to pick your favorite topic in the world from your childhood, say, LA Lakers basketball, and pick out a book that chronicles the teams that you were so passionate about.

You don't need to start with a 500-page book on sales negotiations.

Baby steps, maybe twenty minutes a day. Have fun with it.

Read.

Carry Out

1) Just like the posters in the library say: "Reading Is Fun"

2) Reading varieties of genres will make your brain trigger parts that it is not normally using. It will induce more creative thought out of you on a daily basis.

Chapter 16: LETTUCE WRAPS

Sales stories you just can't make up!
Story #5

I was working with an advertising agency a few years back right when I started at the sports talk station. I had heard some stories that suggested they were a little shifty and difficult to deal with.

But I did not have any problems with them at all. We worked together on two big accounts and got these clients great ideas, they sent me orders, and they were two huge pieces of new business.

I should have known something was wrong when both clients told me directly they had reasonable expectations but knew their budgets weren't huge, so I knew I had to stay grounded about the campaign results.

I guess I thought it was a big order to me, but for them it must have been chump change.

Well, I was wrong.

Here is the long story short on client number one.

He called me after his second month of the campaign and couldn't believe he had received an invoice for a second month's worth of advertising when he had only agreed to two weeks worth.

I thought in my head, "What the hell is he talking about?!?!"

And here is the long story short on client number two.

He called me in September to thank me for a great campaign and to say all of the bills were paid and hopefully we could work together again next year; except he still had bills outstanding for July and August and was set to run September thru November.

I called the agency. It was small, just two people working out of their house, and I received no return phone calls or emails.

Then the phones were cut off.

I have never heard back from either one of them to this day.

But I spoke with both of those clients. The one agreed to a two-week campaign for $2,000.00, but the agency sent me an order for $10k.

The other client had agreed with the agency to do three months for $9,000.00, but they sent me an order for $27k!

They lied about how much these clients were running in hopes of getting a better advertising rate on the radio station.

I was in shock and awe. The one client almost went under because he had an extra 10 grand in bills from us he hadn't agreed to but the agency had ordered for him.

We worked it out with both clients and neither was upset with us, because we only did what we had been told and instructed to do from an order standpoint.

But I couldn't believe it. It was right then and there that I realized if you hear something over and over about someone from multiple sources, you should always give that person a chance, but don't be shocked if it turns out to be true.

In this case, the agency was just as shifty and shady as I had been told.

I can't make that up. It was unbelievable.

Please follow the Golden Rule. If you do, I don't think you would ever behave in that manner because you wouldn't want that to happen to you.

Carry Out

1) Follow the Golden Rule.

2) Do not be shady in sales. Just don't. It gives everyone else a bad name in the industry.

Chapter 17: Gluten-Free Buns

Transformations

Now, some people think that transforming yourself would be changing who you are and what you represent.

Since the whole point I am trying to make in this book is that being yourself is one of the most important qualities you need to have day in and day out, that wouldn't make much sense.

What I mean by transformations is probably better put in the words that Brian Solis used in his great book from 2011 called "The End of Business as Usual" when he says over and over that we must "ADAPT OR DIE!" I suggest every business owner or consumer should pick this book up and give it a read.

Transforming the way we do business is one of the most important traits we need to have. That so few do it correctly gives the opportunity for those who do to make greatness in our lives and careers.

Every day society is changing. Technology is evolving. More options are created for how customers use their money and the choices they have.

If you are in sales, marketing, or own a business, then you must be willing, able, and know when to transform the way you sell or market the products you represent.

An aging and stale product is a recipe for failure to hit budget. It is a recipe to fail to meet your clients' goals. It is a recipe to fail to meet the income level you want to attain. It is a recipe to fail to achieve longevity and greatness in your career.

Transforming, when called upon to do so, shows energy, forward thinking, and the ability to be a confident leader in your company and in your industry. Many people, however, are too "proud" or "feel questionable" about certain trends. They refuse to transform themselves, which will inevitably lead to their demise.

Maybe not tomorrow, maybe not next year, but a failure to be open and willing to change the way you operate when it is called upon will eventually keep you from achieving greatness.

There have been drastic changes between when I first entered radio sales in 2005 and how I operate now in 2012. It is amazing to see the changes, learning experiences, and, yes, transformations I have undergone in order to stay at the top of my game.

You must still prospect and perform cold-calling. But now you find introductions through Twitter, contact names through LinkedIn, locations of key decision makers through Facebook and Google. We no longer are forced to cold-call a business out of the Yellow Pages and ask the lady at the front desk, "Can I speak with your advertising manager or marketing director?"

Yet I see and hear every day of people still doing that. It is a waste of precious time. Five minutes searching on the internet can you get a contact name, description of their job, info on how to reach out to them, and perhaps what type of person they really are.

I have done a 180-degree transformation in how I prospect and cold-call for new business. I have not transformed the way I behave and act on those leads. I have transformed and adapted to the new way of prospecting and interacting, and it has benefited me greatly.

Thousands of reps in multiple industries still refuse to go a new route, and their unwillingness to transform the way they operate will eventually cause them growing pains.

The way I have clients reach me has changed. I rarely give out my office number. The cell phone is the way to go. If you are an outside sales rep, it doesn't do much good to give a client a phone number you are in close proximity to only three hours a day. It doesn't make sense and yet I see it happen everywhere.

The way salespeople and business owners must treat their customers, gain insight from what they have to say, and converse with them to come together on an idea has changed, and I have transformed my thinking in that process too.

Very few advertisers and businesses have money to spend just on "radio" or on "TV." They have money to spend on turnkey solutions that will make them a profit for their business. Often I hear "that client doesn't like radio" or "that business doesn't have a radio budget," and people don't try to approach them.

That is bologna. If you have an idea that will make a business a profitable return on what they invest with you, they will have the budget for the product that you represent. It may take more work. It may take killer ideas and extra meetings. It may take several rounds of proving you are REMARKABLE.

I have transformed myself into this process. I have refused to admit that someone just "doesn't do radio" or "doesn't eat hot dogs."

It is an excuse. It is a barrier. It is an objection.

Everywhere we must stop letting barriers, excuses, and objections stand in our way and let the client decide for themselves if our ideas are good enough for them to give us a chance at their business.

Don't let time pass you by. Don't get sloppy and old in the way you operate or do your business.

You don't have to be on Facebook 12 hours a day or tweet 95 messages per hour.

But you do have to transform and adapt your way of thinking. If you sense a way you have been working is no longer viable for your use of time, or is not getting the results you wish to attain, you need an open mind and a willingness to transform yourself.

I have done it multiple times already in a very short career. I attribute a huge part of my success and my ability to keep the ball rolling for my clients and my company to the fact that I have an open mind every day. If I need to adapt or transform something in my routine that doesn't change the way I act as a human being or cross over with my missions and goals of being myself, then I am all for it!

And you should be too.

Brian Solis is right. It is time to adapt or die.

Carry Out

1) Be on the cutting edge and don't get "old school."

2) Don't overdo or get addicted to one way. It will change.

Chapter 18: YELLOW MUSTARD

Sales stories you just can't make up!
Story #6

Convenience

When it comes to how I set up meetings with my clients, I would always like to hear them say, "Mike Rudd just makes it convenient. He will come meet me whenever, wherever. I have a goofy schedule and he makes it work. Others try to make me rework my schedule. Not Mike."

While it is a two-way partnership, I do my best to work for the client. I feel I should go out of the way to make meeting with them much more convenient on their end than it is on my end.

I meet with people after hours, at odd coffee shops across town, in a different city if called for, on an early morning conference call, etc.

I will even go so far as to meet at someone's house. I have had ten to fifteen meetings over the years where I've gone into a stranger's house on the first call, and while some would think it a little strange or intimidating, I am offering the convenience the client needs.

One meeting five years ago almost changed my entire thought process on this, and now I definitely do some research about the person, neighborhood, or at-home business before I walk in those doors!

It was 2006, and I was still working at the classic rock station. We also had a second station in the active rock format (and a third station that played country). Active rock music varies, but can include some of my favorite bands such as Tool, Metallica, and Nine Inch Nails. It can also get much heavier than that and delve into the 80s metal and hair band era.

I was meeting with this guy named Mark who was promoting an all 80s hair band show at a local venue that I will describe simply as the "location where Dimebag Darrell from Pantera was shot on stage by a fan and killed." Needless to say, it was a tragedy but also shows the type of clientele that may show up at a show at their venue.

RIP Dimebag.

When Mark suggested we meet at a local Tim Horton's coffee shop instead of that particular venue, I was more than okay with it.

Mark was normal enough on the first meeting. A pretty typical representation of what you would think a show promoter doing 80s metal and hair band music would look like. He had long hair, was sporting a Guns N Roses T-shirt, rocking a sizable beer belly, etc. He also was a super nice guy.

When we wrapped up our first meeting and had agreed to the commercial schedule he was going to run on our active rock station leading up to the show, the plan was that we would meet again so I could pick up the check and write the spot. He said he lived right down the street and that I could come by and pick up the check that Friday. It was on a major road and he was a very normal guy, so I thought nothing of making another of my "house calls."

Friday came and I pulled up to the address. It was in a huge gap on this major road where there was not another house or business within half a mile. Just a long dirt road leading back to what I assumed was his house. I saw a rickety mailbox about to fall off its post with the address he had given me, so I knew I was in the right place. There were tons of overgrown trees and shrubs, so I couldn't see the house. A "NO TRESPASSING" sign about the size of a teenager hung next to the mailbox as well. But Mark had told me to come over and pick up the check, so I didn't feel I was trespassing. I drove over a quarter mile down the dirt road, a long way if you think you are just going down a driveway.

As I got more nervous and clammy, I started to see dog and cat pet carriers. You know; the ones you load up "man's best friend" or your "kitty cat" in to take them to the vet. They were EVERYWHERE! I counted at least twenty strewn across the yard. Actually, it wasn't a yard; it was the middle of the woods. Toys and boxes and junk were all over the place.

Finally I found the house. This was beyond getting creepy. The house had no windows and looked like it was going to fall apart any day. I finally decided to call Mark on his cell phone to double-check that I wasn't walking into a serial killer's home. It reminded me of a place that Buffalo Bill from *The Silence of the Lambs* would have enjoyed spending time at if he weren't so busy kidnapping women and torturing them in his deceased mother's basement.

Mark answered, and I mentioned something about a lot of dog and cat carriers outside since that was the only thing I could really describe to verify I was at the right location.

He replied, "Great, come on in, man!"

Did Mark and his cult have other plans for me? Was I walking into a trap?

I always try to give people the benefit of the doubt, and I thought it was a pretty silly notion that Mark would pick a radio sales rep that was about the same size as him and without a beer belly as his next possible "target."

I walked into the house. JUNK. CEILING-HIGH PILES OF JUNK everywhere.

The place was small, each room so packed there was no place to move or sit, and it stunk. There were no dogs or cats – strange, considering all of the carriers outside.

I turned the corner and saw some kid, probably 18 or 19, playing the guitar while standing up and smoking something through a sort of gas mask device. He was breathing through it and sounded dead-on Darth Vader when he took each breath.

He nodded at me, and I looked around to the other room where Mark was sitting at a keyboard writing music. He shook my hand and said hello. We told a few jokes, and he gave me a CD with the spot on it. He also wrote me a personal check for the full amount.

I thanked him for the business, walked by Darth Vader, (I never did see any dogs and cats that would have explained all of the pet carriers) and he waved goodbye. As I walked out, I looked around the structure some more. He could have killed me. There wasn't a soul that would have heard my screams.

As I got into my car he hollered at me "Oh, by the way, sorry about the mess, man. I just had to move my parents into a nursing home and I am staying here for a few months to clean it up!"

Wait a minute?!?!

Mark wasn't a serial killer! Mark wasn't a torture chamber expert.

It had all been explained to me and was later summed up when the hit TV show on A&E came out two or three years later. Mark's parents were HOARDERS!!!

I drove off relieved!

Never assume people are who they are. That will still go down as the creepiest place I have ever visited in Columbus. And I still don't know who or what the guy with the guitar and gas mask was, why they had all those pet carriers and no animals, and it sure didn't appear Mark was making much headway in cleaning out his hoarder parents' mess of a house.

But I was safe, and Mark was normal!

And I heard his 80s hair band show sold a ton of tickets, so good for him! Everyone has their niche in life.

Carry Out

1) Mark's parents' house would have made for an awesome episode of "Hoarders."

2) I bet the odds are 50/50 Mark still lives there.

Chapter 19: BARBEQUE SAUCE

Positivity and the power of positive thought.

I know what you may be thinking when you read this. Don't bore me or tell me that I need to be more fun and happy all the time. This is business and business is hard. Life is hard and to get to the top of the business world, as a business owner or especially in a cutthroat industry like sales, I am going to have to step on some necks, make some noise, and get stressed out about it.

I am here to tell you not that you are wrong. I believe all people have their way to enjoy their days and their life and if they truly are happy one way, this book is not here to tell you that you are wrong and to change.

I am here to tell you, though, that the process of daily positive thinking, letting negative things roll off your shoulders, and just a lot more daily positive interactions with people have gone a long way to create great momentum in my career.

Stresses are something we honestly create. We convince ourselves we need to have a new car, or a golf club membership, that we need to do this and save money for that.

90% of stress in life ultimately boils down to money. Even if it is relationship stress or family stress, I would be willing to bet if you dig deep enough into the situation, it comes down to money.

Stress and the desire/need for more money for more things creates negative thoughts in our minds and won't let us truly be ourselves and see how remarkable we can become, because we are always worrying about something!

"Keeping up with the Joneses" and the "Rat Race" are very real in society. Part of that is society's habit of not letting people enjoy each day for what it is. To not worry about what is down the road. We're convinced we need to save XXX amount of dollars for a house, a car, tuition, which making us always look ahead instead of staying in the moment.

I have worked very hard on this for a number of years, and I have found that positive thought, taking one day at a time, enjoying what you do throughout each day, and generally going out of your way to be kind to people will make you feel better inside.

When you feel better inside, you will be happier to jump out of bed for the day, for your career, for your family. Eventually it will push you farther in your career toward where you want to go. If you don't get bogged down by the minutiae of always looking to what is next, you can enjoy the best thing of all: RIGHT NOW!

One of my favorite authors/writers/creative role models is Tim Ferriss. Tim has written two of my ten favorite books, *The Four Hour Work Week* and *The Four Hour Body*. Tim recently posted on his website and blog two commencement speech videos. The first is the famous speech Steve Jobs gave at Stanford in 2005, the "Stay Hungry Stay Foolish" speech. Incredible stuff that I recommend everyone watches!

The second speech was given by a man named Neil Gaiman, who created a popular comic book called "The Sandman" in the 90s. I had never heard of Neil or the Sandman comic, but Tim highly recommended everyone watch the commencement speech he gave to the University of the Arts this past year. It is also a must-see video and can be found on Youtube or by searching past posts of Tim's at his website www.fourhourworkweek.com/blog.

Two takeaways stuck out to me from Neil's speech:

1) He found that anything he ever did in life solely for money never worked out and he hardly ever made money at it.

2) Stephen King told him when his comic book first became popular to make sure he enjoyed the ride. Neil said it was the greatest advice he ever got, but it took him almost 15 years to begin following it. He was always worried about the next deadline, the next idea, the next chapter. Now he says he enjoys each moment for what it is worth.

I am sitting at my kitchen table and having already seen the sunrise this morning, am enjoying a dazzling cup of loose-leaf green tea. I've said good morning and given my wife a kiss on the cheek; and am very much enjoying writing this chapter right now.

And I haven't even started getting ready for my day, according to the pundits!

But the pundits may not always be correct. This is my day, everything I do in my day I try to enjoy and I try to only do things I want to do. And I thank God for the moment that has been given to me.

How does positivity and positive thinking wrap back into this?

If as we rise out of bed, proclaim to ourselves it is going to be a wonderful day, and simply enjoy all of the little moments that life brings, you will be shocked at how much fun even a Monday can be!

When you start telling people good morning even if they are looking down, waving at friends instead of driving by because you are in a rush to get to work, or instead of saying "fine" when asked how your day is going, replying with a "wonderful" or "awesome," you would be surprised to see how much more positivity comes rolling into your life each and every day.

Helping others more in need than you makes you realize how lucky you are, and the act of helping them build their lives back up will make you a more positive thinker as well.

We can't control traffic.

Repeat to yourself: You can't control traffic.

If you live in Ohio or somewhere else cold in the winter, you can't control the weather.

Repeat to yourself: You can't control the weather.

There are so many opportunities in the world every day that could use our help. Neighborhoods and families locally, countries and regions globally, and really everywhere you look, there is a place that could use some help.

If we spend our time bogging ourselves down with the big picture, always worrying about our next budget, our next goal, how bad traffic was, you can't believe it rained on your birthday, BLAH BLAH BLAH BLAH, then it will be a long, negative, stressful life.

Jobs will be hard and unfair. Commission sales just won't work out for you. That's what you will tell the people at the neighborhood barbecue after you quit yet another gig. Even though, in truth, you went into that job everyday with your head down and didn't say good morning to any co-workers, you were in a bad mood because you got stuck in traffic, and you didn't call enough prospects or dream clients because you felt you didn't have what they were looking for that day.

We can only control ourselves. I am not here to change you. Only to give the advice of what has helped me get where I am today. I am nobody in the whole grand scheme of life, please know that. But I am somebody in that I am loving life and am passionate about what I do every day when I wake up. Mondays are just as fun as Fridays for me. I enjoy before, during, and after work equally.

Of course, there are things that happen in my life I wish did not happen. There are wars I want to end, hungry kids in Columbus I want to feed, friends that have cancer I want to be cured, family members and friends that passed before it was their time, and peace and happiness I wish every person in the entire world could experience on a daily basis.

But not even the president can change all of that with a snap of a finger.

All I can do is change my thinking, my actions, my thoughts, and each and every day do my part to achieve what I think gives me greatest pleasure and happiness, and to look back on my life and say, "I did something. I helped make a change."

One final note here; I can already see the anonymous bloggers saying, "Well, he is in sales so he cares about money" or "Give up all of your stuff and donate all your possessions to the poor then."

That is not what I am saying. If I did that, I wouldn't be able to help try to make a change in my community. I do what I do because I love working with remarkable people. My boss and people in my company are extraordinary human beings who are contributing far greater to the good of the world than the stresses of it.

I work with clients who are trying to live their dreams of owning their own businesses, and each and every day I feel that I am on the front lines with them trying to help them make achieve those dreams.

I got into this industry because I think it is fun to meet and talk with people of all walks of life. I am passionate about this sector and feel there are a lot of game-changing remarkable people who want the same thing as I do, and that is why I do what I do.

The second that would ever change, I would rethink everything. But I don't think it will and I don't ever think about it.

You know why?

Positivity and the power of positive thought. I tell myself everything is going to work out and it does.

You play the game in the rat race and you will find yourself constantly behind, stressed out, upset from a lack of praise, in a traffic jam, and pissed because it rained on your 38th birthday.

You make the choice. I chose, and the power of positivity has been a game changer for my entire career and life on and off the work court.

Carry Out

1) Everything that happens in life you can put a positive spin on.

2) When someone says, "Not bad for a Monday," reply with: "Hell, yeah, Mondays rule!"

Chapter 20: KETCHUP

Sales stories you just can't make up!
Story #7

Tee Times

Oh, yes. Golf and sales. Sales and golf. They just go hand in hand with each other. In fact, during the summer, I barely even go to the office. All of my work just gets done over handshakes, shanks and hooks, and cocktails on the golf course.

What a sport it is!

WRONG! I play golf during work about once a summer.

"I have actually golfed with clients, only a few times and only with ones I really consider to be friends just as much as clients. And business is never brought up. Any business that needs to be discussed can be done at one of our offices or beforehand." One of my favorite clients, RP, the owner of a local advertising agency, told me that once years ago and it struck a chord of honesty and integrity with me.

But I do have a great tee time golf sales story!

It was about a year into working at the hot dog stand. Things were rolling along in our busiest time of the year, fall quarter, when the new school year officially kicked off. The weather was still hot, kids still had money, and we were out on football game days, so it was always our best quarter of the year.

We had three hot dog carts at the time. I ran one, Eric, the owner, ran one, and Ryan ran the third one. My good friend James loaded up all of our coolers, product, etc. and would drop off and pick up at headquarters each day so we had as light a cart as possible when we physically pushed the carts about one mile from the Ohio Union to our spots each morning and then back each afternoon. Couple in running every night and walking to class, I was in superb shape when I worked that job, but that hot dog cart was still heavy as all hell to push every day.

Ryan, similar to the guy whose job I received after he was let go at Boss Doggs, had quite the passion for the Bier Stube, the local watering hole about four blocks down on the OSU campus. Ryan actually lived right next door to it, so it fit in really well.

Ryan was a good guy but he would get so mad if one little thing didn't work on the hot dog stand and it cost him say $20 in commission.

Totally understandable as a college student, right?!

Well, Ryan was in his mid-40s and older than Eric, so it was a bit of a stretch.

He also didn't have many hobbies outside the hot dog stand other than reading, watching sports, and hanging out at the Bier Stube.

I was shocked and excited for him when one Wednesday morning before we pushed out he approached me and said he would give me $10 of his tips each Wednesday if I cleaned up his cart at the end of the day. (Cleaning our cart consisted of a 20 to 30 minute process of scrubbing, washing, putting stuff away, and so forth.)

I had class to get to, I told him, and wasn't sure if I could swing it. But he begged me, because he had a tee time at 3:30 p.m. every Wednesday afternoon for the rest of fall quarter.

I was happy he had found a new hobby and was being active. And I wouldn't be the only student twenty minutes late to that marketing class. At least I was going to it, which can't be said of all college students when it comes to attending classes.

The extra $10 cash was definitely worth the 20 to 30 minutes of extra time when you think about it on an hourly scale as well. I was rushing through cleaning both of our carts after the second week and I asked Ryan how he'd played the week before?

Ryan replied, "I shot 8 under on 9 holes."

I was stunned!

Ryan was one of the best golfers I had ever met. Instantly I thought about entering golf scrambles with big money prizes with my two high-school pals Wunder and Silber (the two best golfers I know) and show up with Ryan – the four of us could make a killing. They wouldn't need me, but it was my idea so I should still be on the team and get an even split, I figured.

That idea never came to fruition but the next week Ryan told me he shot an 11 under on 18 holes, his best round yet! He told me he was winning the league, obviously.

He would have been winning PGA tour events with scores like those.

I thought to myself, what a great deal. I am making basically what I would make in an extra 30 minutes in commission in sales out at the hot dog stand from him for doing a little extra clean-up and he may be working toward a second career as a golf pro at a country club!

WHEN IT IS TOO GOOD TO BE TRUE, IT USUALLY IS.

After about four or five Wednesdays I was scrubbing down Ryan's cart and Eric, the owner, finally said to me, "Why do you scrub Ryan's stuff down every Wednesday? Did you lose a bet with him or something?"

I told Eric about how Ryan was paying me, and while I was getting to my class about 40 minutes late I didn't mind because I was glad I was helping him out, and I told him about how great of a golfer Ryan was!

Eric started howling with laughter.

Tears dripping down his face, he finally said to me between laughs, "Ryan's tee time isn't really on a golf course, you idiot!"

Eric then went onto to explain that Ryan wasn't a golfer at all. Well, depending on who you ask and what criteria they use.

Ryan plays Golden Tee.

Ryan plays Golden Tee at the Bier Stube every Wednesday with the same three guys. They do keep score in a league format, and the scores Ryan was reporting to me were correct.

But they were from the Golden Tee Arcade game!

I asked him about it the next day, and he said he thought I knew what he was talking about. I laughed and told him, "Just so you know, when somebody says they have a tee time; that actually means they are physically going to play on the golf course."

Sales 101: If the story seems to be good to be true, such as a non-athlete working a hot dog cart breaking PGA tour course records, it probably isn't true.

Ryan was giving me $10 for me to miss the first half of one of my core marketing classes so he could go play video games and pretend like it was an actual sport while he was getting sauced with his other 40-year-old buddies at the Bier Stube.

I politely told Ryan I would have to let him resume cleaning his cart because I was doing it mainly to help him get out and be active. He grumbled something about hoping he could push the tee time back with his buddies. As if there were another group lining up at the Bier Stube at 4:30 p.m. pushing those guys to get off the Golden Tee machine!

Tee times. Ha!

Carry Out

1) Ryan was really good at Golden Tee, though.

2) Be curious, ask questions, and never assume! (Words of wisdom from my awesome boss Todd!)

Chapter 21: MAYONNAISE

Don't get complacent

If there is to be long-term success in my field and similar fields, then a resistance to being complacent is necessary. I know this is something that some would consider to be a great trait in all industries, and I agree. But when we are looking at, say, ten or eleven traits needed for-long term greatness, a lack of complacency has to be included.

Every sale, every month, every budget, every year, there are opportunities for us to become complacent in our industry. I have seen it happen numerous times to people who are just as good, if not better than I am, when it comes to the actual selling part of our job. This is different than maintaining a full funnel because this falls under the category of not taking any business for granted. Of not allowing any awards or pats on the back to take away your sense of urgency every morning when you go into your job.

In sales there are so many budgets and so many calls that people very often fall into the trap of achieving a monthly or yearly goal and becoming complacent. They feel they have reached the top of the mountain, and all they need to do is continue to circle around the mountain to stay on top of it.

The sales industry doesn't work that way. There is no top of the mountain.

We can always go higher, and to be truly amazing in sales, marketing, your own business, there is no end until you decide it is. If you want to truly remain in control of your own destiny and possible greatness, then you need to set goals that make the mountain have no peak.

You also need to be ready to set goals that most would laugh at even the thought of trying to achieve them. We never know how far we will go unless we push ourselves to go further than our brains and bodies would under normal conditions.

I read a recent article about an ultra marathoner (someone running distances in a day that most will never run in their entire life) who transformed himself in his 30s from a couch potato who was depressed into one of the greatest athletes in the entire world.

Once he had done this and began to compete in ultra races around the world, he grew weary of winning them all and competing just against himself.

He was not complacent, though. So he set his own goals. He chose a mountain that had no peak. And he went out.

Last year he completed FIVE Ironman's in ONE week in Hawaii. He did one on each of the five Hawaiian Islands, to boot.

It is a record, I guess. I say I "guess" it is a record because no one else has so much as attempted it.

If he has no one that even thinks they can attempt to break what he did, then it is beyond a record. It is his personal milestone, his personal mission statement.

That is showing a lack of complacency.

For over 84 months I have been given ample opportunities while others have thrown in the growth towel and traded it in for a complacency towel. They felt safe, and able to nestle into the top of the so-called mountain, and decided to just start walking around on top.

Complacency towels should be reserved for retirement.

Don't let the bug bite you. When you think you have achieved everything possible, then think again.

Sit down and start brainstorming how far you can go. What else can you add to your repertoire?

Learning a foreign language to compete internationally in your industry?

Learning to play a musical instrument to impress your musically driven clients?

Taking a series of public speaking classes to improve your closing ratio?

There is so much more than this.

The bottom line is: just because you blow away goals, projections, or revenues, it does not mean it is time to stand still and begin patting yourself on the back.

Those who choose to circle the mountain and wear their complacency towel around their neck while they do so are much more likely to trip on a pebble and slip down to the bottom of the trail much faster and harder than those storming ahead to the mountain with no peak with a growth towel draped over their head and an innate sense of purpose for getting better everyday.

Complacency is boring. That means you have reached the end of the frontier.

We should never be done improving who we are.

Throw complacency in the trash can.

Carry Out

1) Complacency sucks!

2) Learn new things to combat complacency.

3) Don't let anything go to your head.

Chapter 22: HOT SAUCE

Sales stories you just can't make up!
Story #8

Sometimes it isn't even the sales call or the marketing meeting that makes something so funny or worth retelling. Once in a while it is nothing more than a great story about the name of the person themselves.

I was working at the classic rock station when we had a sales contest on the country stations we also represented. For 60 days we held a contest to see who could write the most new business on the country stations. At the end of the contest, the winner would get a billing account on the station that was signed to a two-year contract that had just started and was billing $3k per month for the next 24 months!

It was a pretty good prize. And it could easily be the biggest account I had on the country station.

I had struggled for quite some time selling the country station, and I viewed this as a challenge and an opportunity to prove myself.

I wound up winning the contest and the account by a narrow margin over my friend Steve.

Ross called me into the office and presented me with the account. The lady who was my main contact is what we call in the advertising world a "media buyer." The media buyer is the one part of the hit TV series "Mad Men" that is sort of left out. But the media buyer is a very important piece of the relationship you build with an ad agency, because he or she is the first person you will meet or be in contact with. From there you need to dig much deeper in the agency past that single contact.

The media buyer lady's name was Rhonda Bronson-Bronson.

I repeat Bronson-Bronson.

I told Ross that must be a misprint he had written on the manila folder with the account information. He told me he was pretty sure that was it, but to find out for myself.

I thought Ross was wrong. Who would have two identical names hyphenated together?!?!

Mike Rudd-Rudd

It does have a very interesting ring to it.

Well, I called her, and she answered with a wonderful and engaging voice, "Rhonda Bronson-Bronson. How are you doing today?"

And that is the end of the story.

I found out through someone else at the agency that she hyphenated her maiden name when she got married. The catch was she married a man with the same last name as hers!

And she still legally hyphenated it. Hysterical, if you ask me.

I wonder what Bronson-Bronson thinks.

This story was told first hand by the author of this book Mike Rudd-Rudd.

Carry Out

1) Please don't do that if you are a woman and find yourself in the same situation.

Chapter 23: BACON BITS

Check your ego at the door.

This will go against what you read in many sales, marketing, self-improvement, and business books. But I believe that a huge reason I have been able to motivate myself continually to achieve goals, keep my funnel full, and strive to be remarkable is that I feel I need to, and I do, check my ego at the door.

The sales industry is a difficult profession in which to check your ego at the door. Often because of all the praise that can bestowed upon you for closing a huge deal or having a record year in sales you can start to think you are better than you are and you begin to let the ego get inflated. The same can happen to a business owner who experiences their first year of record growth after years of struggling to break even.

Ego inflation can cause us to lose our motivation. We begin to build ourselves up as something that we aren't. We begin to convince ourselves that we are almost invincible and immune to what is going on in the outside world.

We think we have become extraordinary sellers or business owners. It causes a drop in the prospecting we do.

We put less thought into the questions we ask our clients, when we could dig around and find true problems with their business we can really help them with. When we let our ego in the door and inflate ourselves every day, we think asking a client questions during the sales process is unnecessary because we already know all of the answers.

The ability to check your ego at the door keeps you focused on the true tasks at hand. Those tasks are providing outstanding service for your clients and coming up with marketing plans that focus on people who truly need your product or idea. As a business owner, it helps you keep a goal of making your community better rather than just your wallet.

When our ego gets in the way, it affects our fire and burning desire to achieve greatness, because our ego is so large that we feel we are already great and there is no need to try.

There is a fine line between being confident and well-spoken, which is a trait that we really need, and being cocky and loud-mouthed. The difference between the two really comes down to your ego.

When you don't have an ego, you are smart and attentive about the product you represent. Your focus is on helping make the team around you better, your clients more informed, and helping them all achieve greater results.

When you have an ego, you wind up walking around pounding your chest most of the day. You speak about how much your clients love you, how they are all getting great results and are happy with your service, yet it has been a long time since you have done anything for them other than take them out to lunch to gloat about how well you are doing.

Having no ego is where the ability to achieve long-term success increases and can occur.

If you can find the fine line between being a hungry, smart, confident sales and marketing specialist and not stray into the cocky, blowhard, know-everything-about-everyone, then you will push yourself to the top of the field.

When you don't have an ego, you don't care about the awards and accolades. At the end of the day a piece of paper, a plaque, or an announcement means nothing. You know in your heart and in your client's words whether you are doing a great job, and so long as you love what you do and are being fairly compensated for it; that is all that matters.

I don't try to hit my budgets so that my boss can send out a mass email saying how great of a job I did. But that is because I checked my ego at the door.

There is no satisfaction in that for me. It is not about me and it never will be about me. What is important to me? It is my clients. They deserve the press, the features, all of the great results.

Beyond the clients, we need to be leaders on our work teams (if you work at a big enough company) where you don't care who gets patted on the back for getting the job done. As a great team member and a true leader you don't need to be told by others how great a job you did on a recent project or that the team couldn't exist without you.

The reason is twofold: 1) You already know how important you are in your heart and that is enough for you. It is a trait of confidence, not a trait of cockiness. 2) You did it because you want greatness for everyone else on your staff and at your company.

Even in the cutthroat world of sales where some will say you need an ego to correctly represent your product to sell to the customer, I will say the exact opposite. It is more important to be open, yourself, honest, and fun with your clients than to come in and proclaim outstanding features of your product and put a "hard sell" on them.

If you are a creator of art and want the best for your family, your clients, your team members, your community, your country, and ultimately this world, then we all need to check our egos at the door and leave them there for our entire career.

The more we can all work together and respect each other for who we are without contending that we are better, or we should get this or that, the more we will be able to make memorable projects and creations to help better all of us.

And that is what it truly comes down to. Nobody will remember your plaques. Nobody will remember your trophies. Nobody will remember all those "pats on the back."

They will remember how you were able to navigate a team of immensely diverse people, work seamlessly together, and create a project with an end result that helped a client achieve great results. They will remember how you passed all of the congratulations onto your team members instead of taking the credit for yourself.

They will remember how you fought for your clients and your community and helped them create art.

Create your legacy. Some things that we value as important to us will be gone weeks from now. Instead, choose greatness. To do that put ego in the trash can outside and walk into the door that will vault you to the next level of being a true superior human being who will be remembered for years to come!

Carry Out

1) The best of the best don't think about being the best. They just outperform everyone else.

2) Take a compliment, but don't take the ego trip that goes with it.

Chapter 24: CREAM CHEESE

Sales stories you just can't make up!
Story #9

Entertaining clients

A lot of folks who aren't in the media or sales industry like to think (partly because rumors spread and partly because those in the industry like to make them think this) that our day involves prospecting and order-entering in the morning, then in the afternoon and evening it is off to the golf course, happy hour, or steakhouse! Entertain those clients around the clock! Buy them stuff and they will buy stuff from you in return!

This is hardly the case.

But entertaining is part of the gig and there are times when I have clients who would like to take me or my co-workers out in thanks for the job we have been doing for them.

A few years ago I signed up a new client who had not been a big fan of radio.

But we worked through an idea that he loved and it seemed pretty likely it would get him the results he needed and a profit well above the investment he was going to be making each month with the station.

He is a great guy to work with and a week or two before the program began he wanted to take me and some other people from the station who had helped in the process out to a nice dinner as a thank you. He said it would be on him, no questions asked.

I begged and pleaded before we went out to let this one be on me. He, after all, had just signed a great contract and it was going to be one of my top twenty or so accounts on the station.

But he insisted that this was his way of getting to know us better and thanking us for what we both felt would be a long-term and wonderful partnership. I finally conceded, knowing I wasn't going to be able to convince him otherwise.

We went to the steakhouse around 6:00 p.m. There were three of us from the station. He arrived with a co-worker, and the five of us probably had two or three glasses of high-end red wine each.

Then all of the sudden five more guys from his company showed up, and we split two more bottles of high-end white wine.

As we proceeded to our table it was already past 8:00 p.m., and two or three more guys showed up for dinner. As we sat down for dinner, there were about a dozen of us in all. And his co workers were ordering the hell out of drinks!

We were having a great time, including the client.

But it was getting expensive. We all had steaks or fish, appetizers galore, and a ton of a la carte items to go with our filets or tuna. (Actually, I don't like steak very much and I was the only person at one of the nicest steakhouses in Columbus to order tuna. Just to set the record straight if you were wondering who on earth would order tuna instead of a filet mignon at a fine steakhouse when they weren't paying for it. That is two thumbs pointed directly backwards at me. "This guy!")

Wine and fine liquors were all being consumed and some of his buddies then decided to order us shots.

I couldn't believe it.

I felt bad because I knew my client was going to pick this whole check up and there wasn't a thing anyone else could say to him that would dissuade him from doing so. Besides, we were at a point where there wasn't enough room on my credit card to pick it up, so I was just going with the flow.

We each had two double shots of the best tequila I had ever tried. It was incredible. Later I found out those shots were thirty dollars a piece. You get the idea.

I left at 11:30 p.m. that night and there were still five or so of them there having post-dinner cocktails they probably didn't need.

It had to be a $3,000.00 tab including tip when it was all said and done. But I don't know for sure.

But he had insisted and it was his thank you and his way of treating his co-workers and his new partner in radio.

We were all very thankful.

Apparently, he got into a little trouble though when his wife looked at the credit card bill.

I am not 100% sure how the conversation went down or how she found out. But a month or two later I was meeting with her, and she mentioned something along the lines of: "Boy, you and your friends had a good time that night! Don't make that a weekly thing!"

She was more joking about it than anything. But I think her husband got cornered by her and, as most men who have been questioned by their wives know, he might have fumbled the story a tad.

When I say that, I mean he might have mentioned that I was the one who initiated the tequila shots and I was the one who had brought some of my friends from the office along, not the other way around!

I let it slide off and didn't mention that if it was up to me that night it would have been four of us, two bottles of wine, and I would have paid for it.

Every once in a while she still jokes to me that if I am going to go out to the steakhouse again with them to please just give her some advance notice.

The moral of the story is, gentlemen; don't run up a $3,000.00 tab on wine, tequila, steak, and one piece of tuna on the credit card that both you and your wife get the bill for.

That is a dinner you save your up cash up for and keep in a shoe box hidden out of sight and out of mind, then pay that sucker so there is no trace left when you exit!

Some might assume that because I am in sales I have an experience like this entertaining with clients every week of the year.

Not true. We really do work much more than we play and entertain.

Carry Out

1) That was the best and most expensive tequila I ever drank.

Chapter 25: OYSTER CRACKERS

There is no "I" in team. But there still is the hunger to be the absolute best within that team.

Sales is a personal game. Sales is a competitive game. Marketing is a do-or-die game. Entrepreneurship is a round-the-clock game. Being a C-level executive is a stressful game.

Sometimes when we begin to associate ourselves with words like these ("personal," "competitive," "stressful," "do-or-die," "round-the-clock") we begin to feel like it is an us-against-the-world mentality.

We will make it on our own. We don't need anybody other than our clients, our hard work, and our dedication.

Me Me Me Me.

It doesn't work.

To ultimately achieve greatness, and going back to my common theme of not only surviving but thriving, we have to come to the realization that there is no "I" in team.

It is not just us.

To best position ourselves for long-term success we have to find the wins in our teammates and our co-workers to make it to the top.

This is difficult for some because we still have to have the hunger to be the best, not only on our individual team or company, but in the entire state, region, country, or world!

Finding the balance between 100% all-in team players who rely on the strengths of their co-workers and team members but also can find the way to do that while being the most competitive person on the team is a very delicate slope.

To find the middle ground you have to have some of the traits I have spoken about in past chapters. Trust in your teammates and co-workers come from your ability to check your ego at the door.

To find the middle ground you have to be able to be confident in your abilities, to believe you are remarkable and you are the best, yet you know you can't do it without the help of all of those involved.

The more I have relied and trusted my teammates as my career has evolved the better I have become.

I learned this at the hot dog stand, another great takeaway that I was able to use from that job in launching my professional career.

When I started at the hot dog stand, I tried to do it all on my own and I wasn't utilizing all of Eric and Ohio State's help. When I finally began to let go some and rely more on my change-makers, my boss, the resources Ohio State was able to offer, my friend James, who dropped all of my food coolers off in the morning, and my brother Tony, who would pick them up on a daily basis, I finally began to see high exponential growth in my sales.

I realized that we were all in it together. We were a team. It wasn't just me. I didn't operate my hot dog stand on my own. I was the one selling but not the only one who made the wheels turn. The desire to be the best and be hungry never went away; in fact, it only increased. But the knowledge that the most rewarding and most fun way to the top was being an all-encompassed team player is what vaulted the hot dog stand and my sales there to levels that Eric and I didn't think or know could be achieved at that particular stand.

It happens in sports as well.

Many times we see a star NBA or NFL player have that drive to be the absolute best. But not until they release some control and begin to rely more on their teammates and realize that they can't do it alone do they make it to championship heights.

Peyton Manning didn't win a Super Bowl until he had full trust in Dominic Rhodes and Joseph Addai to be great running backs capable of complementing his passing game.

Shaquille O'Neal put up stats and MVP awards galore for the Orlando Magic and the LA Lakers, but it wasn't until he fully trusted in his new Lakers coach Phil Jackson and young guard Kobe Bryant to help him get there together that he begin to win NBA titles.

Shaq and Peyton's desire and hunger to be the best did not disappear when they began to trust their teammates and know that they couldn't do it alone. They just finally realized there is no "I" in team. We have to be able to fully embrace being on a team and love the atmosphere of it in order to achieve greatness.

Being on a great team also pushes you to heights you don't realize you can reach on your own. Great team members encourage you; they invigorate you to push you farther than you would make yourself go on your own. They have a desire and a hunger to be the best as well, most likely. But working in a positive and team-building atmosphere with great, remarkable, highly intelligent people will only push you farther up the mountain. (The mountain you want to climb will have no peak. You never want be satisfied with reaching the top and circling around it. You want to always be climbing.)

Teammates can pick you up when you are down. When you start to doubt yourself, when you start to hear that voice in your head telling you that you can't do it, that's when teammates can hold you up, give you a kick in the rear end, and motivate you to get back to where you need and want to go.

That is why we need to have a belief in our team, in our co-workers, in our employees.

When you are on a team but believe it is only about you is when the walls begin to crumble. It may be a slow deterioration, but it will happen if selfish, back-stabbing behavior occurs within a team and company atmosphere.

You may be able to survive in an environment like this, but remember this book is here to make you great. If you are reading this book you are already good at what you do (or you are my family member). This book is about traits and qualities of greatness we can apply to our current situation and make us become remarkable, unstoppable, and achieve greatness.

Lead your team. Let your team help you. Be the best on your team. Be challenged by your team. Trust your team. Tell your team the truth.

Do this and the rest will be easier, more fun, and much more rewarding.

And your clients will thank you for it, because you will be better at what you do for them. And that is why we are all here, or should be.

Carry Out

1) You can be competitive with your co-workers and still a great teammate.

2) Everybody belongs on the team; don't single anyone out.

Chapter 26: TZATZIKI

Sales stories that you just can't make up
Story #10

My final sales story is more of a tale for inspiration and what truly makes my job as enjoyable as it is.

All of my sales calls and meetings and presentations are stories you just can't make up. You know why? Because they are all a beginning or a continuation or a culmination of the creative and hard work I, my clients, and my teammates have put in together to come up with a solution or idea that our clients will love and hopefully their customers will love more.

You can't make up any of these stories because every meeting is an original in and of itself.

Every client has different needs. Different behavior patterns of their customers. Different company structures they have to deal with in order to get programs pushed through. All of these differences present potential opportunities and roadblocks that are different from one client to the next.

It is a new day every single day. No matter how much you plan or try to figure out what is going to happen there is always something – mostly good, once in a while stressful – that comes up that you must combat or work on to ensure forward movement of a project or idea.

We work together. We meet together. We build together. We grow together. And with the right mindset we prosper together and make customers happy together.

That doesn't get to happen in all industries and in all walks of life.

There is unfortunately a large number of people out there who have very little control or thought process in what they are asked to do everyday in their careers. Very little of the outcome or end product is based on their input and their work.

For those that want it that way, that is wonderful. They should continue to do what they want and if it brings them happiness, keep on keeping on.

But there are also a large percentage who want and wish to have more thought and more input. They want to be more than a clock-in and clock-out career person. And for those people I say figure out a way to go find and achieve those dreams.

If you want more out of your career than what you are getting now, you can change it. You have to seek out what you love and what is possible and go do it.

It doesn't have to be a life-altering event or a 180-degree flip from what you are doing. But if you want to have something more than what you are receiving, then there is a means to the end.

As for me, it truly is an honor and a privilege to work with all of the clients I have worked with over the years. From the early customers at the hot dog stand and my internships, to the great people I worked with at the classic rock station, to my current ones in the sports marketing world.

No two days are the same.

Every day is a new opportunity to help put an imprint on a business, on the community, and make someone out there feel special and smile.

We all work for different reasons and motivations. But in the end you will find if you do what you truly love, you will worry less about the paycheck and more about what you are representing. The good news is often that the paycheck will increase when you do what you love because you will find yourself giving more time and dedication to it. Unless you go into a pure social work or charity sector, that may call for a pay cut, but I am sure you won't mind nor be surprised by it. However, if you decide to do that, you have already made the decision that serving is the most important thing you can do. And that is wonderful.

As I have made fun of my own antics thus far in this book and shared tales of a few of my more wild and unbelievable sales calls and meetings over the years, I know this. That is why I love this line of work. I have exciting and weird stories to tell. I have stories that are funny and engaging, I hope.

They are stories that make me laugh at the end of the day and put me in a good mood from the moment I get out of bed until the second I fall asleep with my glasses still on trying to stay awake for one of those 10:30 p.m. West Coast NBA Games. (I mean seriously, how great must the West Coast be for sporting event tip-offs? I would never fall asleep at halftimes if I lived out there.)

In concluding my sales stories that you just can't make up, I say this. We are creating something so special, so memorable, so customizable that it is different for each and every meeting and client I have.

We are giving something back to the customer. Something that is fun and engaging. Something that is worthwhile to consider purchasing if they have the money and the need.

And while not every salesperson, business owner, accountant, CEO, hot dog worker, or radio station promotions director, may have this mindset now, I believe going forward more and more people will and more and more people should.

It is a pride and happiness thing.

Love what you do.

Have so much fun doing it that people won't be able to make up stories about what you do because what you do is so truly unique that unless they experience it firsthand they can't grasp the magic that goes on in your life on a day-to-day basis.

For that I am thankful and lucky. My clients I hope feel the same way, ditto for their customers.

Some will call this story #10 of calls that I can't make up. I call it story # infinity because every single person every single day has their own story to tell and they simply can't be retold without experiencing it on your own.

Every day is a day that can't be made up, because I won't know the amazing occurrences that will happen until I am sitting right there experiencing them.

Carry Out

1) No one in sales would have the success they have without great clients.

2) Sales or owning a business truly is one of the most diversified jobs day-to-day that you can have. It changes hourly in terms of what you is expected of you and need to tackle.

Chapter 27: POTATO CHIP CRUMBS

Personal branding

Branding may be the hottest buzz word being thrown around in the digital era, but every single person has a different definition for themselves of what it means.

Then there is the term of "personal branding," which has even more definitions. It is even more unclear as to what it stands for, and depending on the person, region, or time of day can have multiple different meanings.

I will explain here what I feel "personal branding" really is and what I have done and why it has helped me.

The abilities that we have in the digital era to stand out as sellers, owners, marketers, and executives are unbelievable opportunities that the generations before us did not have.

Personal branding to me is simply "showing your value to others and standing out amongst the crowd by being yourself and showing everyone what that person is. All of the time."

What? By just acting like yourself you can have a distinct brand? Then why is it so important and one of the soaring buzz words of the digital era?

All of these are good questions.

It was late 2009 and I had been doing sports marketing and sales at the station for almost a year and a half. Sales were good and projections were looking up. But there was no wow factor, I felt, to what I was doing beyond my service and my products. I was not offering value to people beyond what they were paying.

I wanted to make a leap to the next level to ensure I was showing positive benefits to my clients, and even strangers, to demonstrate what I was offering at the sports station was unlike what anyone else offered in the market or quite frankly even in the state.

I began to scour my brain and think of ways I could do this when I simply stumbled upon a book. A book that gave me the answers to what I wanted to do and begin my own version and journey of "personal branding." I read *Why Now is the Time to Crush It!* by Gary Vaynerchuk, and it was one of the biggest eye openers in terms of leading the way for what I wanted to do that I had come across in quite some time. Gary is one of my favorite authors and speakers/bloggers, and this book gave me what I was looking for.

To give a quick snapshot, Gary essentially talks about finally cashing in on your passion and doing what you love instead of working at a place where you don't love what you are doing. He talks about how to make money from writing a blog, promoting it through Twitter, Facebook and other social networking sites.

I wasn't leaving my day job. Because I felt I was and still am at a place where I am cashing in on my passion. But a blog, a personal brand, could help make me an expert in my current career. Offering free content to my clients and anyone who stumbles upon my blog would be the way to show them that YES I do more for my people and offer more value than anyone else. So please give me a chance to meet with you to earn your business.

It was my opportunity to strive for greatness! And I thank Gary for that book to this day.

Thus began my own journey of personal branding.

Depending on who you ask, personal branding is about getting high search returns on google, having X amount of Twitter followers, a large number of LIKES on your Facebook page, etc. That is not what I set out to do nor is it what I feel is necessary for you to begin doing yourself as you seek to go from surviving to thriving and achieving greatness.

I felt that to really go and set yourself apart you simply needed to be yourself. I had read so many blogs and Twitter feeds in my first few years exploring that world that it seemed many people were forcing content and not saying what they truly felt or what they wanted to speak on. If I was myself, then I would stand out. If my own personality and actions truly shined through in my own personal branding, then that is what would make me stand out.

I bought the domain name www.marketingfunwithmike.com, launched a Twitter account and Facebook fan page, and I was off.

I wrote and I wrote and I wrote.

Looking back on it, the first few months were confusing as all hell. What I set out to do, being myself, wasn't happening. I was trying to force marketing lingo and tactics that were difficult to understand at times, and if you weren't very interested in that specific area of business, there was no reason for you to read it. One post a week turned into one every two weeks, and I felt that I was struggling for content.

Marketing Fun With Mike was an extension of who I was in terms of the domain name. I smile, I enjoy myself, and I love to just talk and hang out with family, friends, and complete strangers. But what I was putting onto the site was not jiving with that, so I felt I was not totally launching my personal brand. It is a process, though, and doesn't occur overnight. I thought instead of trying to force content, I should just keep reading others, tweeting when I had valuable information, and think a little more deeply about where I wanted my writing to go to enhance who I really was and thus create my personal brand in the marketplace.

While I struggled through the writing process in the first year or two, I will say it was an immediate door opener with potential clients. The fact that I had even gone out and purchased a domain name and was trying to write impressed enough prospects that I knew it was worth my time to keep working at it and I just had to hone in on what I really wanted to say and supply people with. I never thought about giving it up, only taking more time to think about the direction that it needed and I wanted it to go in. It was a real opportunity and a real potential game changer for my business, I felt, and it was not to be thrown away.

Finally it dawned on me. Epiphany time!
Just because I work in sports marketing and the blog's core content is about marketing does not mean that every single post had to be strictly about marketing. If I was setting out to be myself, I realized I never just spoke to people about only marketing all of the time in real life. So why I would do it on my blog?!?!

A light bulb had gone off in my head. It was when my wife and I returned from our honeymoon in June of 2011 that I started writing. All of the sudden my one post every three weeks turned into two or three posts per week. My interactions went up, my Twitter followers started multiplying daily, I was having calls with younger professionals who wanted my help, and I was reaching out to people I now considered mentors.

Why?

Why after a year and a half of struggling to write could I all of the sudden quadruple my posts, become a contributing writer for SportsNetworker.com, and begin and finish a book over the past year and a half?

It was because I let go. I unleashed who I truly am 100% on the blog and on social media, and that's where it led me. It was easy after that. The process was difficult, but it was and still is worth it. I don't have ten million followers on Twitter, I don't have two million subscribers to my blog. But what I do have is this: people I interact with everyday who tell my how much they enjoy what I'm putting out there. I also have a group of people who I read and thank for their writing to return the good karma. Together I finally created for myself what the digital experts like to dub a "personal brand."

My personal brand is just an extension of myself. And that is all it needs to be. You need to let your inner self shine out.

If you don't like to write, launch a YouTube video blog. If you don't like to be seen, launch a podcast audio blog. If you have attention deficit disorder and can't write very long, launch a twitter account where you give valuable opinions and insights about your industry in 140 characters or less!

Over the next twenty to thirty years in business the word "brand" will be used with more variety and confusion than any other word in the sector, so it is very important what you decide your version of a personal brand is.

To me personal branding was an opportunity to showcase who I really am and how I really act to potential prospects and clients. The person that I am on all of those social media outlets and on my blog is the same person and acts the same way as when I am with my family, close friends, colleagues, strangers, and anyone I run into. My goal is to treat everyone with the same respect as I would a close friend or family member. No more and no less. That is my personal brand.

To give free, valuable information to my clients and anyone else who would like to read it. Because it is worth it and it is fun.

My clients are making hefty investments with me, and they deserve more value than just having great ideas, wonderful customer service, and on-time results. They deserve to be treated to a value greater than that. And that is what Marketing Fun With Mike and all it encompasses brings to the table, in my opinion.

What it has offered me is the same offer waiting for you today: the opportunity to put yourself on a higher level of the playing field than every other business owner, salesperson, marketing manager, creative director, etc. in your industry.

And you can do it almost for free. You need to have desire and want and be willing to put in extra time that others in your industry are not. But if you are reading this book and you truly want to grasp the theme of thriving in your industry over the next few decades, then you know what you need to do.

Don't be fake and don't force content. Don't try to gain to simply gain.

Be yourself, be engaging, be valuable, set yourself apart, have fun, and enjoy yourself.

That is what creating a personal brand is about. It is that simple, in my eyes. No rocket science. Just the experiences that taught you about your industry (HOT DOGS), a tad of added industry experience (A LITTLE MARKETING), and enjoying yourself every day while doing it (A LOT OF FUN!).

Carry Out

1) No need to worry about the quantity of your tweets or followers/fans. It's about the quality and the value you give them.

2) A personal brand is just an extension of your personality and showing everyone that you aren't one way at work and totally different at home.

Chapter 28: COLESLAW

Let's take a to-go order of hot dogs and see what we came up with, what I think I and all of us need going forward over the coming decades to be great in our ever-changing business world.

1) Remarkable level of customer service.

2) Love and have true passion for the product you represent.

3) An overflowing funnel of potential business.

4) Read, read, read.

5) Positivity in all aspects of life every day.

6) Transform and develop yourself when needed.

7) Lack of complacency.

8) Check your ego at the door.

9) Embrace being a teammate and a leader.

10) Learn what your "personal brand" is.

That is the list that I came up with.

As I look through it sitting at my kitchen table this morning I almost laugh out loud.

This list is not exactly rocket science and it really is simple in nature. (That would explain the low price on Amazon, wouldn't it?!)

But then when I really think about it, I am very proud of this list and I love this list because this is what I use everyday. And thousands of other successful people in this country and other countries are using similar lists everyday and achieving long-term success in their industries.

When we achieve long-term success we don't get stuck in ruts. We have a chance to improve our lives, and our client's lives, and it gives us the time and opportunity to help with our family, friends, neighborhoods, and countries problems and issues.

And that is what life is really all about. Trying to better the world in which we live. It is about sharing your enjoyment of this beautiful place. Giving and not receiving. It is about the process of trying to let others have the opportunity to be as happy as you are everyday.

This list is not and was not, you will notice, a how-to on closing techniques for sales. It was not a tutorial on cold-calling opening lines.
It is rather a mission statement. It is a collection of thoughts and traits that when used by themselves may not be very effective. But when put together and shaken up, they truly have the capability to create some amazing effects.

This is my mission statement. Not just for today but for tomorrow and next year and the next decade.

I honestly believe that this list can and will withstand the test of time. No matter how many new products, distribution channels, pricing options, etc. come out, this list works.

It gives us the core competencies we can apply and use to thrive in our industries. I feel that business owners, C-level executives, salespeople, and marketing departments can most benefit, but if you look at this list, it really can with a tweak or two every day applied to so many more industries.

It is inside all of us.

It is about being ourselves. I know that every single person is wired a little differently, but when you get down to the inside core of what makes us get up everyday, we all have the same thing in common. Every single human being in this world wants to be themselves, they want to be happy, they want to be excited for each day, and they want to do something that makes them so pumped up every morning they can't wait to start doing it.

Thirty, forty, or fifty years ago only about 10% of the population got to do this, I would venture to estimate. That number is changing. It is still far from where it should be, but it is growing every day. Past 30% now, I would say, and within another 30 or 40 years past 50%.

Why?

We don't have a choice. Terrorist attacks, recessions, and global development have changed the way in which business works. The nine to five cushy jobs with the corner office for being nothing but loyal are disappearing at a rapid rate.

We will thrive by doing what we love. By doing what makes us and those around us happy. By being ourselves.

You don't believe me?

Go look at websites like kickstarter.com and fiverr.com. Walk around your neighborhood and your city and see how many new local shops and businesses are popping up. Talk to your family members and friends and you will hear more stories of "I may try this" or "I'm going to go work there."

One of the goals on my "things to do before I die" list was to write a book. That is now done. I couldn't have done it thirty years ago without quitting my day job and hoping against hope that some publisher would feel the need to market a book with a guy in a hot dog costume on the front cover. But it is possible now. Everything is possible now.

I want to write an article for Bill Simmons unbelievable ESPN off-shoot website Grantland.com. I have just started to email and tweet to him because his information is out there. I am going to make it happen someday soon. But even if it doesn't happen or I change my mind, a guy like that wasn't so easily accessible thirty years ago. Now he is just a mouse click away.

We have to sit down and figure out what we want to do, what we want out of life, where we want it to take us, and start trying to go there. The second all of us start doing that and using this list, or the best form of it depending on the industry, is the second road rage, bitterness over weather, blaming the boss, street fights in bars, etc. start to go away.

It is not a kumbaya mission here. It is a mission to do what you have the opportunity to do and do what we all should do. We were told to put our heads down and listen up at work, get through it and by the time you were sixty-five years old, you could have a nice pension and finally enjoy yourself for ten or twenty years of retirement before you die. Those days are over!

Partly because those places that told us that are getting rid of their pensions, which aren't coming back, and they're firing the people they told to keep their heads down and shut up.

Why not live your whole life on semi-retirement? Doing something you love while doing everything you want.

We need, to quote one of my favorite authors and business mentors, Seth Godin, "to become linchpins." Linchpins are indispensable workers. Not head down, keep quiet, and pray you don't get fired workers.

We have to become mission workers. My mission statement is listed above in ten simple steps for my current job and industry. I personally believe that along with my drive, the act of being myself – and hot dogs – are what have enabled to me to love every day of my current job, and my past jobs, and that they will create a long-term successful partnership with my company and my clients for years to come.

Speaking of the devil, let's get back to hot dogs. We talked about marketing and fun for long enough the past few chapters.

Carry Out

1) Not all ten points are for everyone. Take the best ones with what already works for you and mix in where you need and want to.

2) Send me an email at mike@marketingfunwithmike.com with your favorite and most beneficial points from my top ten list and any you would like to add.

Chapter 29: VINEGAR

I didn't know any more than the next guy about sales, running a business, or what it took to be extra focused and dedicated when I started working at the hot dog stand. But, to come full circle, it didn't take long to teach me and put me at a launching point for a career in giving, customer serving, and thanking.

The hot dog stand was a 101 basic level class at first and eventually an advance placement degree in sales and entrepreneurialism that everyone would benefit in going through if it were actually a class and a degree.

Nowadays in school and then work we are taught something, we are told to regurgitate, to memorize and recite. Rinse and repeat. We are judged on what we can spit back out in school on tests rather than applying what we have learned to on-the-cusp thinking and everyday applications.

I am very thankful for all of the teachers and schooling I have had over the years. But I think getting thrown into a real-life situation while still in college gave me the knowledge and expertise needed to really succeed. It was also a very early eye opener in my career in just how hard you have to work. Sometimes upon graduation first-time jobs are given to students who experience a complete culture shock to the business lifestyle and the post-student life.

Learning all of this while still in school is of extreme benefit. Because it doesn't matter how many *A*'s you get, what your GPA is, or how many clubs you are in once you start in the real world. It all disappears and you are left with your mind, heart, desire, and knowledge to apply what you have and what you strive to gain more of. You are on your own.

The hot dog stand taught me that above all else in a job, above all of the duties, all of the politics, you just need to be kind. You need to be genuine. When it is a rainy day, smile instead of complaining about the weather.

Every day is a gift in this world and too many times we look past all of the beautiful little moments that are passing right before our eyes. Because we are worried or stressed about something that happened months before or won't occur for a long time.

Boss Doggs and the hot dog stand gave me the opportunity to slow time down every day and fully grasp and enjoy these moments and teach me how important they are. I would be out on Ohio State's campus early in the morning on a summer day when no one was out and about, and it was like watching the sunrise. It gave me moments of clarity and time to reflect and enjoy the small moments.

Think about it for a minute. Why do we really work? We do it to support our families, to make money, because we have to, because society wants us to. We do it for all sorts of different reasons. But if our work week consists of 45 hours, and sleeping takes up 49 hours, then we are left with 56 hours of life to enjoy. That's not much time. (I always say we can sleep less but it does eventually catch up to you.) If we spend half of those 56 hours worried and getting upset about work and the other half running errands and doing stuff that will get us ahead so we don't have to mess with it during the work week, where does that leave us?

It leaves us in a place that is probably sad and stressful, without the joys of everyday life.

I encourage everyone, no matter how hard or easy it may be, to really do some searching and find a career, a path, a passion that you can enjoy during your work time, after and pre-work time, and weekends all the same. To relish in everything that happens every day. The bottom line is that one day is only one day, unless you waste it or don't get to enjoy it. Then it is just a speck of dust that rolled past you in the wind that you were unable to do anything special with.

The hot dog stand came at the right time and at the right place in my life. I was already reinvigorated with life and very passionate about the degree I was pursuing and was having a great time with the life that I was leading. The hot dog stand gave me the necessary learning experience and applications of business, passion, and training that I needed to move my career forward.

For that I will always be grateful and I will never forget my time there.

Are you sitting there asking yourself, "That's great buddy, but unfortunately I can't get a job at a hot dog stand"? Then I am glad to deliver the news that I feel we all have a "hot dog stand" somewhere in our life. We will all have that job, that volunteer gig, that friend, complete stranger, or that moment in time when our own hot dog stand tips us toward doing something with our passion instead of just going through the motions.

For me it was an actual job selling hot dogs, but it is different for everybody. It can be as short term as a weekend seminar with motivational public speakers that gets you to switch into an industry you love. It can be as long term as teaming up with a friend on a Tuesday night building project for two years that convinces you to finally open that kitchen remodeling company you had dreamed about starting.

For myself the hot dog stand said to me: "You love people, you love working with people. You love sports, you love music. Never settle for anything less at a job that you don't adore doing every day. Don't ever work at a job or in a career you dislike. And if anyone tells you that life or work sucks, then ignore them because it isn't true!"

For you, your hot dog stand may tell you something else. But if you keep your eyes open, you will have that moment or period of time in your life when you are doing something that makes you so happy, so excited, so grateful for every day on this earth that you will want to find a way to do that type of job or career for the rest of your life.

Keep your eyes open for your "hot dog stand." It is already right in front of you or will be there soon.

Carry Out

1) The hot dog stand is your key to happiness and enjoyment in work.

2) Work for what you love; not just to get paid.

Dessert

This is the after-dinner course, you could say. It is the dessert, the final thoughts, the wrap-up, the conclusion, etc.

I'd wanted to write a book for a few years. But I didn't want to write a book just to cross it off my "What do you want to before you die?" list. (Though there is a great book with the same name by the Buried Life and I highly recommend it.)

If I had wanted to simply do that, I would have just put all of my blogs into a collage and turned it into one large book. People do that, and there is no shame in it.

But I wanted to inspire. I wanted to tell a story from the heart and what I thought would help others who were searching for something more both in life and in their careers.

I have been very lucky and very fortunate over the years to work with incredible people, but I will say that I have tried to seek out working with those people. I don't want to settle for anything less. I don't want to settle for an "average day" or an "okay month."

I want it to be pure excitement and fun around the clock. I think we deserve to have this happen and the only thing stopping us is ourselves.

Go find your own hot dog cart. And turn that into your passion. Maybe you are already working at one; that's where my points and thoughts about what you need to thrive and not just survive will come in handy. After you have the "hot dogs" and "a little marketing," the rest of it is just being yourself, whatever it is you want to be, and the way you are, and that will create in your own world "a lot of fun."

That's all business is, and life really. Finding something you love, adding your own tidbits of knowledge to it, and then enjoying what you do.

Hot Dogs, A Little Marketing, and A Lot of Fun.

I guess I could have put the words "All you need to succeed in business and in life" before that part of the title because that's all I really set out to do and talk about in this book.

I hope I helped. I hope I made you smile. I hope I made you laugh. I hope I made you learn some new ways to work and to live and to love.

That's all I wanted to do.
I am confident I did actually. And if I did, put this book down now because it is over and go find your own "hot dogs, a little marketing, and a lot of fun" and make a career and a life out of it!

Carry Out

1) Thank you so much for reading and making it to the final page! I appreciate the support and would love to hear from you on your thoughts. Email me at mike@marketingfunwithmike.com and we can set up a time to meet face to face or talk on the phone as well if you prefer. THANK YOU!

Dedication and Acknowledgments

I would like to dedicate this book first and foremost to my loving wife Jill. You put up with my shenanigans on a daily basis and mean the world to me! Every day is simply a pleasure to be able to spend it with you. Together we will laugh hard and have fun until we are both off of this Earth.

Also to my parents (my mother who gets an extra shout out for both being a wonderful Mom and for doing a book edit of this during her first summer of retirement from high school English) who had to put up with my shenanigans for 18 years before Jill did and shaped me into who I have become, thank you and I love you. You have always let me see how far my dreams will take me and I was never told I couldn't accomplish anything before I even attempted it. And I know you will continue that support for the rest of our lives.

To my grandparents Ed and Rose who are no longer with us but watching over me and were the ones who really taught me that no matter what life throws at you being kind and genuinely nice to people no matter what will help you and being mean to people will only hurt you. To my grandparents Bill and Eileen who I hope I make proud every day and taught me to never stop exploring and learning.

To my brother Tony who is out doing a 100-mile run or something absolutely crazy right now in the world of tri-athletes, keep rocking!

To God for giving us everything on this beautiful earth to enjoy every day and in no way could there be a more wonderful place and time to put me on this fine Earth, and for that I am grateful every day.

It is also impossible to have a greater extended family (including the in-laws' side, I swear!), group of life-long friends growing up in grade school in Kenwood (Hornets Pride), high school in Cincinnati at Moeller and Mount Notre Dame (Go Big Moe!), all of the wonderful people I met at college at Ohio State from all over both Ohio and the country (O H…), and all of my friends I have met since then as a permanent resident in Columbus and a quasi resident of Le Mars, Iowa. Every single one of you along the way has meant so much to me and please never lose touch, you know I won't let you anyway!

A special thanks to those who helped me in the process of writing this book. Don "The Idea Guy" Snyder for his book foreword, encouragement, publishing ideas and so much more in the process. It would not be what it is if not for you. Check him out at www.dontheideaguy.com to see his magic in full force.

To my awesome editor-in-chief, my Aunt Sharon! If you like food and need a fresh idea head over to her blog at www.eggplanttogo.blogspot.com. She was a huge help on my editing and helped get rid of plenty of word fillers and punctuation errors!

To all of my teachers, mentors, and role models that I have had along the way in school and in my career who pushed me to go farther than I thought I could. Especially Eric Clark, Todd Markieweicz, Karac Ruleau, Bob Crable, Charity Kirtley, Mitchell Bowles, Ross Wagner, Joe Hardin, Kathy Karnap, Dan Shannon, Mike Kearney, Steve Klonne, Roger Blackwell, and Randy Malloy.

And to all of the authors, bloggers, and digital peeps out there who provide me with my personal daily reading material and motivation for what I do, thanks for sharing your passion. Thank you for the fire, the ideas, and the daily motivation. I learn so much from all of you every day.

This book is also dedicated to everyone else who is out there doing something they love and enjoying life for the great experience it truly is. And if you aren't, this book is dedicated to you too and I hope you will find your own hot dog stand! I know you will if you keep searching.

Perform random acts of kindness, treat everyone as though they are your best friend, smile randomly and often, and of course CARPE DIEM.

About the author:

Mike Rudd is a sports marketing specialist who works at 97.1 The Fan Sports Talk Radio in Columbus, home of the Ohio State Buckeyes on the radio. He lives in German Village in Columbus and loves in his free time to explore the city, the country, and the world! He also enjoys fun times with his family and friends, working out and playing sports, helping make the world a better place in his way, reading, writing, coaching, and, if you know him, talking. Yes, he loves to talk!

If you are interested in seeing if Mike can help with your business locally in Columbus at 97.1 The Fan, or if you are interested in booking Mike for a speaking appearance or seminar at your business or company anywhere in the world to add some "hot dogs" to your company, or if you just want to chat about the book or make fun of it, you can contact him at mike@marketingfunwithmike.com.

Check Mike's website out for speaking engagement info and for updated blog posts at www.marketingfunwithmike.com. He can be found on Twitter at http://twitter.com/marketingmiker and on Facebook at www.facebook.com/marketingfunwithmike

Made in the USA
San Bernardino, CA
18 December 2012